SIDE HUSTLE

How Squares like us in the real world can improve our Bottom Line and compete with the Sharps in the world of sports gambling

BRAD TAYLOR

Copyright © 2023 Brad Taylor

All rights reserved. No part of this book may be reproduced, stored in a retrievable system or transmitted, in any form or by any means without prior written consent of the publisher, except in the case of brief quotations, embodied reviews and articles.

Cover Design by: Jennifer Wright
Published by: The Author's Way Publishing

ISBN: 979-8-8692-1345-7

Find Brad at:
https://www.wlxg.com/podcast/the-bottom-weekend-line/

ACKNOWLEDGEMENTS

First and foremost, I believe in God. Exactly the first thing you expected to read in this book, right? If that makes you close this book and put it back on the shelf, I understand. But we are all just trying to pick winners and cash tickets here. Nothing more. We all have that goal in common when it comes to sports gambling. Like everyone else, I have experienced highs and lows in life. There were days when I felt like my faith was all that I had. I prayed to emerge from the dark days and flourish. I am very grateful for all those who saw me through those difficult times. My family is down to one person, a mother for which I am so thankful that I still have. From growing up in a small town in Madison County, Kentucky, to my decades of walking the "mean streets" of Atlanta, and now back in Lexington, Kentucky, I've seen and experienced things I never thought I would when I was a kid. All those people and experiences are gifts from God. I would enjoy naming everyone and singling all my wonderful friends out for your enduring friendships and love over the years, but I don't have enough room for all the names. Those names will be called out in the next book, *Side Hustle 2: Electric Boogaloo*. Laugh if you must, but there will be a second book. Maybe the name needs work for copyright purposes only!

Having said that, my relationship with God, and faith in Him through good and bad times, means more to me than anything. I'm very fortunate and grateful for the life that He has mercifully given me. All of us are given gifts and talents. Finding our niche in life by using them can be the difficult part. Sometimes, we must keep up our **Side Hustle** mentality until we do.

As fate would have it in this world, guilt can play tricks on us as well as sports gamblers. My faith in God often made me question if I should be betting on sports in the first place. I have even spoken with religious leaders over the years, asking about it. **Bottom Line**: there is no passage in The Bible that says it's a sin to bet. That's not to say Moses has a 16-team parlay on the first full day of the NCAA Tournament every March, but it's like anything else in life: moderation.

Sports gambling is taking over the United States of America. I can sit here and type out all the numbers of how this country gambles this amount of money every calendar year on sports. But by the time you read this, those numbers will increase to make the current numbers irrelevant. It's everywhere! And believe me when I tell you that the oddsmakers are (and always will be) a step ahead of the bettors. Somehow, we must find a way to fight back! And when I refer to "we," I'm referring to the Squares in the sports gambling world. The Sharps are the Wise Guys in the desert who can turn a profit, and the Squares are people like us who have numerous obstacles in our way before we can turn a profit. That's a big reason why I've taken to writing this book. How do regular people like us compete against the Sharps who bet professionally every day? We don't have the time or faculties to put in all that time and effort! We've got careers, families, obligations, responsibilities, and distractions that make putting hours into handicapping sporting events 365 days a year almost impossible. How do we do it? That's what this book is about more than anything else.

I do have to acknowledge my employer, or I won't be employed much longer. I would be remiss if I didn't thank ESPN Radio WLXG

SIDE HUSTLE

92.5 FM and 1300 AM in Lexington, Kentucky. I walked into LM Communications in 2020, just pre-COVID, and demanded that they give me a radio show! In Lexington, home of The Big Blue Nation and The University of Kentucky, every fan boy in the state thinks they can do a radio show better than the professionals who are already on the air. But LM could hear what I was saying. I wasn't some fanboy trying to have a local team pep rally show. I was trying to say that sports gambling was coming, and it's better to be ahead of the curve than behind it. Of course, COVID-19 didn't exactly hasten the process. But here we are a few years later, and we really are ahead of the curve! I am very grateful to everyone at LM Communications for giving me the opportunity and a platform to do "sports talk from a handicapping perspective." I'm very proud to have the first daily radio sports handicapping show in the state of Kentucky. They took a chance and bet on me when nobody else would. Hopefully they will continue to cash that ticket.

And I want to thank the listeners to my show. I get emails and messages all the time from people who want to voice an opinion of my sports gambling topics. So many of them are complimentary of my work, but there are always the haters. I get it all! For example:

"You don't sound like everybody else, so I don't like you."

"You're not one of us, so I don't like you."

"Nobody cares about sports gambling. Talk about something else!"

"Stop talking about gambling and talk about that sophomore in high school who can't even drive yet and that might be coming to school here!"

"You always pick the local team to lose! Why are you so mean?"

"Why do you only talk about games that have betting lines?"

"You're not a fan of any team? Why should I listen to you?"
"Your show sucks, and you're lucky to have a job!"
"You're fat!"

I'm on the radio! How can people call me fat? I reply to that last one, "Yeah, Phat with a P-H!" You're always going to have haters in life, especially if you are successful. And the more successful someone is, the more people will come out of the shadows and try to bring that person down to their level. Many sports fans are closet "wannabe" sports talk radio hosts anyway. People think you can just roll out of bed and talk by yourself every day, but it's more difficult than it appears. And in my case, I have no co-host, producer, or anyone to help with show prep. If I am silent for 5 seconds, BOOM! People are changing channels immediately. There's more work involved than just rolling off the couch and yapping. But as crazy as it sounds, I'm thankful to be in a position now where the haters make me smile. And for that, I thank you.

I've been a subscriber to Sports Insights for a few years now. It's where I get almost all the numbers that I use (both in this book and in my own handicapping) for historical data involving point spreads and totals. It's also where I experiment with betting systems, and find out which systems work, and which don't. There's a difference between trends and systems, but we will discuss this later. The **Bottom Line** is that Sports Insights has been an invaluable source of sports gambling information for me, and I cannot recommend their services more. I am not affiliated with them, so this is just me giving a personal endorsement based on the results that I've had using their help. If you enjoy the data and statistical information in this book, check out the people at Sports Insights who provided a lot of it. The data that I pulled from Sports Insights was taken in July of 2023, during the MLB All-Star Break, vacation time for the dedicated sports gambler.

There's a glossary at the end of this book that reviews much of the terminology used here, but here's the 2 main ones:

Sharps (Pros): Longtime successful sports bettors that bet big and use value and data. They can turn a profit in the long term. Probably not you.

Squares (Joes): Part-time unsuccessful sports bettors that bet bigger than they should and have no game plan. They usually don't turn a profit long term or have staying power. Probably you.

Sharps will look at this book and laugh. I don't blame them. This book is aimed at people like you and me: Squares who will be able to take some things from this book and make themselves a little better at sports gambling.

With that, I wish you the very best in your sports gambling endeavors. And as always, may the winners be yours.....

SIDE HUSTLE

SIDE HUSTLE

TABLE OF CONTENTS

ACKNOWLEDGEMENTS	3
INTRODUCTION	11
PART I GETTING YOUR MIND STRAIGHT	**17**
1 GETTING STARTED	19
2 RISK TAKING	21
3 TOP 5 QUALITIES OF A SUCCESSFUL SPORTS GAMBLER	25
4 THE MENTAL GAME	29
5 EXPECTATIONS	32
6 REINVENTING YOURSELF:	36
7 DAVID vs. GOLIATH	41
8 TAKING WHAT THE GAME GIVES YOU:	45
9 ACCOUNTABILITY	54
10 THE ULTIMATE LESSON	58
11 DELUSION	77
12 STAYING THE COURSE	82
13 THE *JEOPARDY!* DILEMMA	89
14 SQUARE THINKING vs. SHARP THINKING:	93
15 DONT BE A PELPHREY	107
16 THE PRIVATE VICTORIES IN LIFE	113

17 FADING THE PUBLIC	117
18 DON'T BE A FAN	120
19 SELF-AWARENESS	126
20 TRAPS	131
21 THE PROLINE EFFECT	134
22 POSITIVE REINFORCEMENT	137
23 LIGHTNING ROUND	141
PART II LET'S MAKE SOME MONEY!	***143***
THE PRE-GAME PLAN	145
RECOGNIZING WINNERS	152
THE FALLACY OF 52.38%	155
LET'S MAKE SOME BETS!	156
LOOK FOR MARKET SIGNS	161
TRENDS AND SYSTEMS	163
WHAT TO PLAY	167
MAKING THE BETS	172
HOW WE PLAY THE GAMES	174
PART III THE SPORTS BETTING CALENDAR	***219***
CONCLUSION What did we learn?	***253***
GLOSSARY	257

SIDE HUSTLE

INTRODUCTION

There's a lot of books out there about sports gambling. Who is this **Side Hustle** Guy and why should I listen to him?

My name is Brad Taylor. I am currently a sports talk radio host in Lexington, Kentucky. The show is called *"The **Bottom Line** with Brad Taylor."* And the tagline is "sports talk from a handicapping perspective." That's simply a nice way of saying I talk about sports gambling. I'm going to handicap these games anyway! Why not talk about it on the radio?

Let's get a few things straight right off the bat: I'm not some millionaire sports bettor than cashes 6-figure tickets on a regular basis and lives on a yacht in the ocean. In addition, I have family, a career (not sports gambling), obligations, responsibilities, and distractions that come first and foremost before sports gambling. In other words, I live in the real world just like you.

Not everyone can quit their jobs, move out to Nevada, and take up sports gambling as a career. We have families, and they are always first. There were plenty of times I just wanted to head out to the desert on my own. Not only would I have lost my butt miserably in my younger days, but my family would've been beside themselves. And how would that look on the resume'? Person A ditched their career and their family to move out west to be a professional sports gambler. After saying that out loud, it just doesn't seem like a smart investment.

This book is for The Average Joe, the everyday man, and the guy who has other priorities in life. How do we compete in this new sports gambling world where the Sharps have plenty of advantages over the Squares?

Before we get started, let's get some things straight. Here are the qualifications why you should NOT listen to me or read this book:

I am not a professional sports gambler. It's a **Side Hustle** done when I make time.

I have a career, family obligations, distractions, and responsibilities that keep sports gambling from being the top priority in my life.

I was terrible at every sport I ever tried to play, and never played any sports (unless you count Wiffle Ball, Nerf Football, Nintendo RBI Baseball, and Tecmo Bowl, all of which I performed at a Hall of Fame level). If you're one of those jocks that won't listen to someone because "they never played the game," then this isn't the book for you.

I have no close relationships with anyone involved with any professional or major college sports team, so I don't have "inside information."

I don't watch every game in every sport so that I can gain more knowledge of the contests in which I'm investing.

I'm not a fan of any individual team or person in the sports world.

To be honest, I've learned that those last 2 choices have become positive traits in my line of thinking.

We reference Sharps and Squares a lot in this book. The Sharps have something that a lot of us don't have: time and peace! I'm a Square! I don't have any inside information. I don't have 8-12 hours a day to do nothing but handicap games, although sometimes I wish I did. And my main career is not depending on sports gambling to pay the bills. As the book title says, sports gambling is my **Side Hustle**. And hopefully, you also see sports gambling as something on the side, and not your main source of income. But I enjoy trying to solve the mystery in every game that asks the daily burning question, "Who is the right side?" It's like watching *Murder, She Wrote* reruns. Or even going back to the unintentionally comedic *Walker, Texas Ranger* where Chuck Norris pulled off miracles every episode, but that's another story for another day (or for Conan O'Brien's Walker, Texas Ranger Lever from back in the day, a comedy masterpiece).

But how do we, the Squares, compete in this new world of sports gambling? The Sharps do this all day, and every day. We've got to get up and go to our jobs, pick up kids, go to soccer games, get the groceries, and get home in time to watch *Wheel of Fortune* and *Jeopardy!* with the family. The Sharps don't have to deal with such foolishness!

As the name of this book implies, **Side Hustle**, sports gambling is not my top priority. Sure, I put a lot of time and effort into sports gambling. But there are a lot of things in life that are more important. Most of the gambling books that are out here on the market don't address the fact that we live in the real world. And most gambling books out there paint this beautiful picture of living in the desert mansion with pool side bottle service every day while enjoying the lavish luxuries of cashing more tickets than anyone. But that's a bunch of crap. As Squares, we can't devote 8-12 hours a day trying to handicap sporting events like most of the professionals or Wise Guys in the Desert, as we like to call them. People like us can't sacrifice everything to bet on ballgames. We need to figure out our own ways of getting our small piece of the huge sports gambling pie. We can, but it's difficult. We are inherently at a disadvantage in many ways.

Most of us have a family and a career. Unfortunately, not many of us can just throw our normal lives away and start a sports gambling career on a dime. You want to talk about pressure? Try having $500 to your name and having $1,000 on an NFL game in 1990? That's pressure.

So why should you listen to me instead of someone who claims to hit 98% of their bets and lives alone on a yacht with several beautiful women who wear nothing but bikinis 24 hours a day? Just because I'm on the radio every day talking about sports gambling certainly doesn't make me, or anyone else in the media, an expert. We lose just like everyone else. Now that I've convinced you that I have absolutely no sports gambling credentials whatsoever, here's why you SHOULD listen to me:

I have never had to take time off from sports gambling due to financial reasons (aka haven't gone broke)

I have never had to take time off from sports gambling due to mental reasons (depression from losing)

I've been doing this since the 1980's, long enough to see the ups and downs of what sports gambling can do to a person and a family if not done correctly.

And that's it! I consider myself in the top 5% of sports gamblers in America. Why? Because of those 3 simple reasons. Have you bet on sports in the past? How did it end for you? Did you use up your bankroll with silly wagers towards the end of your run? Did you get upset that you kept losing and couldn't stop the pain? We all go through those moments, as some might call it being "on tilt," and the best in the business can bounce back. For others, it might take more than a minute, if it's possible at all. Granted, it takes discipline and hustle, but it can be done. Every individual sports gambler just must find their niche and routine, which is easier said than done.

Let's summarize the qualifications of the author of this book. Here's a guy that never played sports, doesn't have any connections with anyone associated with a sports franchise or program, and doesn't watch many of the games on which he wagers. Not only that, but this guy also doesn't care who wins or loses these games on which we are betting because he's not a fan. And people are supposed to read this book and take some suggestions from it? Crazy talk!

Look at all the things we have against us trying to become successful sports gamblers? Families, careers, obligations, responsibilities, and distractions. All these things are very important in the real world but hurt us when trying to get our **Side Hustle** on and betting on sports. And who among us can take 8, 10, or even 12 hours a day to handicap games? There are times when I wish that was my life, but I'm still hustling trying to make a living.

As we get started in this book, realize what you're in for if you enter this world of sports gambling. Everything is against us, the bettor. Hitting 50% of your straight bets at the normal –110 juice or vig will send you to the poor house. Not only that, but the minute we start betting in sports, we are at a huge disadvantage to those who have more time in their lives to devote to gathering data and information. Before we begin, we are already at a huge disadvantage. This book will hopefully help in the evening out of the playing field between the Sharps and the Squares. Because believe me, it's a big difference.

SIDE HUSTLE

PART I

GETTING YOUR MIND STRAIGHT

SIDE HUSTLE

1
GETTING STARTED

Is sports gambling for me? Am I able to take risks?

"Brad, how do you still have so much money?" - My childhood friends while playing Monopoly.

I played Monopoly a lot as a kid. And I hated to lose at Monopoly because I was going to be a tycoon when I grew up. When we played at my house, I was always the banker. And if I was the banker, yup, I cheated my tail off. Sneaking a deed in my stack, grabbing a little money here and there, whatever it took to win. When I was banker, I always had a scam that anytime I passed "Go," I always took $300 instead of the $200 I was supposed to take from the bank. It wasn't much, but it added up as the game progressed. But when I went to someone else's house, I couldn't be the boss Monopoly banker and had to play by their rules.

How do I cheat on the road? Easy! Take money from my own Monopoly game to use on the road at someone else's house. I'd just stuff my pockets with Monopoly money and start the game with a loaded bankroll. Granted, I eventually ran out of Monopoly money in my own game. We just started using $1 bills as $100 bills. But from a very early age, it was all about winning. And that's what sports gambling is about too: cashing tickets and The **Bottom Line**!

SIDE HUSTLE

Do you want to do this right? Do you want to cannonball into the deep end of the pool? Or do you want to just dip your big toe into the shallow end and see how you feel?

BREAKING NEWS: sports gambling is very difficult. I cannot stress that enough and will many more times in this book. If we all could do it, we'd all be in the desert picking games every single day. But it's a tough racket. And unlike being the banker in Monopoly, we cannot blatantly and hilariously cheat the sports books. This is Big Boy World.

I handicap games 361 days a year. I take 4 days off in July during the MLB All-Star Game, and it's probably my favorite week of the year to escape the grind! But this is truly my **Side Hustle**. It's a hobby. Some people like to shop, go to movies, or dabble in collectibles, and that's fine. My hobby is trying to pick winners. It's what I enjoy doing, and I don't lose my shirt.

Can you deal with losing money? Can your ego handle losing? Can you bet against your favorite team? Can you bet on your most hated team? Can you not go with the masses and make your own way? These are some of the basic questions that you need to ask yourself before getting involved in sports gambling.

BOTTOM LINE

Before jumping in the sports gambling pool, know that this is an extremely difficult task to make money long term. The media and others can paint this as positively or negatively as possible, but sports gambling is about one thing and one thing only: making a profit. It's not about having a good time or making friends. If you want that, get a dog!

2
RISK TAKING

Walking alone is better than walking amongst the others.

"Adapt or die!" - Former Oakland A's General Manager Billy Beane.

    According to Wikipedia, A 1993 study found no correlation between the use of fuzzy dice and the degree of a driver's reckless driving behavior. I don't believe that for one second! But anytime I saw fuzzy dice hanging from someone's rear-view mirror when I was a kid, I thought of that person as a risk taker and a rebel. And that was someone I wanted to be. Sadly, I don't see them now nearly as much as when I was a kid.

    I haven't always worked in sports talk radio. I have a health care background and spent a couple of decades working in the field in both Atlanta and Kentucky. Most people now think I'm some degenerate gambler who just sits around coming up with moronic clichés with a plate full of bratwurst and salami on the coffee table in front of my couch on a Saturday afternoon watching 15 consecutive hours of sporting events while not taking a shower or brushing my teeth. That couldn't be further from the truth, and it's a terrible stereotype for any sports gambler.

SIDE HUSTLE

Here's a little secret I don't share with a lot of people: I don't watch many games anymore. If I learned anything from the wonderful book *Moneyball* by Michael Lewis, it's that even the Oakland Athletics General Manager (and subject of the book) Billy Beane wouldn't watch games involving his teams so that he wouldn't become biased when it came to roster moves and decisions based on old school ways of thinking. If I'm trying to handicap games, I need to keep a clear mind. If I get all the local teams on TV, and listen to their media wax poetic about them, I'm going to become biased towards them. And that might affect how I invest my money. We cannot have that!

But Beane was one of the ultimate risk takers in sports history. With a low-budget team, losing all its high-priced talent to teams that could afford to pay them, he had to learn a different way to compete. He couldn't approach it the same as the others. He had to make his own way. The only thing he had to lose was his job, one of only 30 like it in the entire sports world. And in this book, we will talk about different ways of handicapping games that most of the Squares don't look at very much.

Currently living in Lexington, Kentucky, I'm surrounded by University of Kentucky fans. If I listened to very local talking head, I'd think Kentucky football and basketball would win every game they've ever played in the history of time, and it's useless to even play these games because Kentucky will win anyway. It's not a slight to the local media, but I try to avoid local opinion-driven talk to be able to keep an unbiased mind when handicapping games. In my personal experience, I became a MUCH better sports handicapper when I watched fewer games emotionally on television and used data to make my decisions instead of what I saw with my own eyes.

SIDE HUSTLE

In my 40's, I was looking to do something different. I had just moved back to Kentucky to help my family, some of which desperately begged me daily to come back and help them. The way they grew up, it was my responsibility to do so no matter what I was doing in my life. So, I moved back to help them. I can take some solace in knowing that I made the final few years for my grandmother and father a little better than if I hadn't. But I was looking to reinvent myself in some way. It's not that I didn't like health care, because I do enjoy helping people. In this new world of health care, it just wasn't as satisfying as it had been in the past.

I decided to take a big risk and pursue sports talk radio. I didn't have years of experience, but I had 2 things that couldn't be seen in the box score: knowledge of my subject matter, and desire to become just a little relevant in the new world of sports gambling. A few years later, here we are. It would have been easy to just keep doing what I was doing, but I wanted something more. It was time to take a risk and adapt or die!

If you're a beginner in sports gambling, I can settle this for you very quickly. The best mental qualities a sports gambler can have in both handicapping games and life itself:

Think contrarian: Always go against the masses.

Don't listen to the opinions of the media or critics.

Work hard and have a passion for this every day.

Faith, family and career always come first.

Try to be the best at this while also staying realistic.

Easy, right? Taking risks changed my life. If that's something you'd like to do too, keep reading.

BOTTOM LINE

It's never too late in life, especially for those willing to take chances. Being a daily sports handicapper can change your life, for better or worse. For those who work hard and with enthusiasm, and have supportive people in their lives, this truly can be a **Side Hustle**. But buyer beware, it's not easy.

3
TOP 5 QUALITIES OF A SUCCESSFUL SPORTS GAMBLER

ESPN Classic is no longer on the air. What a shocker! We don't want to watch old sporting events of which we already know the outcome. You're kidding! We don't live in that world anymore. Don't tell me what happened yesterday! Tell me what's going to happen tonight. In my role as a sports talk radio host, I'm more of a fortune teller than anything these days. Decades ago, we depended on the media personalities and journalists to tell us what happened. Now, we know immediately thanks to modern technology. But the one thing that even technology can't do these days is predict the future.

However, they did have other shows and documentaries on *ESPN Classic* that were watchable at times. One of those shows was called *"Top 5 Reasons You Can't Blame."* Host Brian Kenny would look back at sporting events and look at other reasons why a team lost, or a player choked, other than conventional wisdom that the public believes to be fact. Sounds like a show right up our alley! By the way, Brian Kenny is a great voice to listen to regarding MLB analytics on *The MLB Network*. He wrote an outstanding book a few years ago as well. Although he doesn't discuss actual betting on baseball, his way of thinking and discussing MLB can help you handicap games by looking at the right numbers. I am a big fan of his work, although he hasn't embraced sports betting on air (yet).

What is our fascination with lists and rankings anyway? We obsess in this world, especially the sports world, about lists and rankings. Is Michael Jordan the greatest NBA player ever? Who are your top 5 NFL quarterbacks of all-time? Back in the day, it was "Should Pete Rose be in the Hall of Fame?" How about your Mount Rushmore of anything? That's my sticking point! I've heard a lot of sports talk radio shows over the years ask their callers to "call in and give us your Mount Rushmore of your favorite team!" In doing so, the host is doing nothing more than just telling the listeners that they have done no show prep whatsoever, and I'm just getting a roll of stamps and mailing this one in. It's a terrible topic, but I digress.

But since we love lists and rankings, I might as well fall into line. So, in the spirit of this very good, but now defunct show, I'd like to quickly list my Top 5 Qualities of a Successful Sports Gambler:

5. CASHING TICKETS

What? You thought this was the MOST important? It's not. In fact, so many other things are ahead of just winning and losing bets in the desert. The Squares will proclaim that if they hit 55%, nothing else matters! That's far from the truth! Bettors can win 55% of their bets and still not make a profit due to other correctible factors.

4. ROUTINE

Yes, it's boring. Yes, it's repetitive. It's not flashy like the movies and television want to say it is. But if you can do the same thing daily, it helps tremendously. Finding time in your busy day to handicap games, and getting your action down in a timely fashion, is a big difference maker in the world of sports wagering. Personally, the best handicapping runs I've been on are the ones where I have plenty of time to go over the games and have few interruptions while doing so.

And more importantly, being able to work on them at the same time every day makes a difference. Routine matters, and the quicker you can establish one, the sooner you can see the results.

3. EMOTIONAL RESCUE

The Rolling Stones were slowing down a little bit in the 1980's when I first became aware of them, but this little number tells a story all of us in the sports gambling world need to remember. Don't bet with your hearts, bet with your wallet. How do many Squares lose? They bet what they WANT to see happen, more than what they think will happen. That gets us in trouble and is one of many reasons why they build those billion-dollar palaces in the desert.

2. DAILY DISCIPLINE

This is an everyday gig. It's not an "if I feel like it" today thing. Or a "if I'm not on a losing streak" job either. It's every day. Period. Can you find the time to do it every day? Can you muster up the energy when you don't feel like it? Can you get yourself to the computer when you've lost several days in a row and don't want to face the music that you're a loser?

1. MONEY MANAGEMENT

For my money, no pun intended, Money Management is easily the most important aspect of a successful sports gambler. Many a sports gambler can hit above the magical 52.38% winners, but few of them make a profit. How do we not become one of those winning losers? Here are the basics:

- One bet shouldn't change your life. Never bet more than 5% of your bankroll in one wager. Personally, I bet 1%.

- Bet the same amount on every wager. If you get on a hot streak and increase your bankroll, increasing your bet amounts simply gets you back to even quicker when the cold streak happens (which it always does).
- Never bet lines with juice of more than –110. Laying –115 lines make breaking even much more difficult! It's hard enough to win 52.5% of the time. Laying bigger juice means now you must win over 54%? This makes your job even MORE difficult! No thanks!

Those are a few quick tips that will get you on the road to Money Management victory, which is more important than picking winners.

BOTTOM LINE

There is no perfect way to bet on sports. We all do it differently. There are the high rollers of the world who have runners, move lines, and have inside information. Then, there's us: people just trying to grind out a little profit. And of the Top 5 characteristics of a successful sports gambler, winning bets isn't nearly as important as money management.

4
THE MENTAL GAME

Can you stand the rain?

Storms will come. This we know for sure. Can you stand the rain? - New Edition.

This won't be the last reference to late 80's R&B songs in this book. Was New Edition really sports gamblers? Did Johnny Gill like betting on 3-team teasers? Was every Quiet Storm radio show back in the day just a façade just to calm down the late-night sports gamblers with big bucks on the line? This song could be an anthem for sports gamblers everywhere. I'm going to be as honest as I can when it comes to sports gambling: it's very difficult. People try to do this for months, years, decades, and still lose. Those losing streaks will happen. And when they do, can you stand the rain?

You will lose at sports handicapping. You will lose big. You will think you'll never win again. These are things that all sports gamblers endure, regardless of skill. What measures us is how we react to losing. If you go through a bad week or two, you cannot panic. Keep doing what you're doing. Don't change. In fact, bet just as strong the next day. If you slow down when you're on a losing streak, that's how far behind you will be when you come out of that streak.

It's inevitable. You're not going to win every week. The key is how you respond AFTER the bad week. You're allowed to be mad. You're allowed to get upset. But you should keep an even keep an even keel and stay as balanced as possible, especially to the people in your life. You must be able to put the past in the past and leave it there.

I suffered a severe arm injury in 2018 from falling down a flight of stairs (insert joke here). It was very painful, and I was barely alert for a few days from being on so many painkillers. And with my health background, I try my best to never take painkillers, so to take them I must have been in serious pain. I went through a lot to get my arm back to somewhat normal, including wearing a sling for several weeks and 9 months of rehabilitation. Just after my injury, I went on a bad losing streak. It was the beginning of MLB season, the weather seemed unseasonably cold everywhere in the eastern half of the United States, and I was miserable. Not only that, but I also couldn't even pick my nose correctly, much less a sporting event. You name it: the NCAA Tournament, MLB, NBA, even NHL Playoffs! I went on a torrid losing streak. Usually, I chalk up losing streaks as just a respite before hitting a hot streak, but this one was different. I was hurting. I was on meds. And the streak lasted about 2 weeks, starting immediately after I mangled my arm. I started to wonder aloud, "are these painkillers making me think differently?" "Should I take some time off until I heal a little?" "Is my mangled arm making me a loser?" "Why do some people say their farts don't stink?" All very important questions that I was debating at the time.

After a couple of weeks of non-stop losing, the thought crossed my mind to slow down or even take some time off. But then I remembered what I had learned from doing this for decades and watching others fail: when on a losing streak, keep swinging just as hard the next day. It will come back to you. Sure enough, those 2 weeks or solid losers were followed by several weeks of cashing tickets. If I had changed what I had believed, I would have never got back what I had lost. Lesson learned, once and for all.

The Mental Game is high on the list of importance when it comes to sports gambling. Can you keep a sound mind and body? Can you do this every day just as strong and enthusiastic when on a winning streak or on a losing streak? Can you ignore things going on in the rest of your life to solidly handicap games? If you can answer "yes" to these questions, you're on your way. But as those of us who have done this for a while know very well, it's much easier said than done. Preparing yourself mentally is almost as important as picking winners.

BOTTOM LINE

New Edition had it right back in the day: Can you stand the rain? Storms will come. This we know for sure. Are you mentally prepared to feel like an idiot? Sports gambling can do that for you. Are you mentally prepared to put yourself out there and fail? Sports gambling can do that for you. Are you mentally prepared to have less money today than you did yesterday? Sports gambling can do that for you. And last, but not least, can you deal with making unforced errors on your own that cost you money? Sports gambling is truly a mirror to see who we really are. Don't listen to your self-talk when it comes to losing. It will only tell you things that you shouldn't hear.

5
EXPECTATIONS

You can do it……(maybe)!

"Life is about one thing: relationships" - Dr. Charles Stanley.

"Life is about two things: relationships and expectations." - Brad Taylor.

In my Atlanta days, I attended the church where Dr. Stanley (pictured above) was the pastor. He passed away in 2023, and I was very sad that I didn't get a chance to pay my respects in person. But I did in spirit. I learned a lot of things listening to this man speak, but this line about relationships was one that has stuck with me to this day.

I was always moved when I heard Dr. Stanley speak. I had one friend who knew not to call or text me right after I attended church because I wasn't in a joyful or playful mood at that time. I was always emotional from hearing him speak, and it took me a while to kind of get back into the real world. Hearing him speak was something that helped me in good times and in bad times. May he rest in peace.

Relationships are especially important in life. No matter what phase of life you are experiencing, we ALL need friends. We ALL need connections. Nice people are sometimes given advantages, second chances, and breaks in this world that the not-so-nice people don't get. It all comes back to you, good and bad.

That's great, **Side Hustle** Guy, but how can we equate that to sports gambling? Well, we can't. Relationships with people don't exactly help us pick winners. That's why I've added my little words to the end of Dr. Stanley's much wiser words. I'm certainly not comparing my words to his either, as he was a much better man than I will ever be. But his words are true! What do we have at the end of our lives? Are we thinking about that 10-team parlay 25 years earlier? Or are we thinking about the relationships we had with people along the way? Relationships are more important than cashing tickets, as crazy as that might sound on an NFL Sunday.

People approach me today as the guy on the radio that talks about sports gambling. And let me tell you, it's not a very popular spot 100% of the time. I could pick 99 out of 100 games correctly. Does anything say a word about the 99? Nope. But I get lots of feedback on the 1 game I missed out of 100. It's just human nature. There's nothing you can do about it. Being in Lexington, Kentucky, I often compare it to Kentucky basketball going 38-1 in 2015. The Kentucky fans don't remember the 38, but they sure do remember the 1. You know, the 1 where future NBA superstar Devin Booker didn't play the last 12 minutes of a close game? I'm sorry! I'm just piling on now.

In 2008, Georgia began the college football season as the #1 ranked preseason team in the nation. That team was loaded with talent like future Super Bowl winning quarterback Matthew Stafford, future NFL All-Pro receiver A.J. Green, and that season's Heisman Trophy preseason favorite, Knowshon Moreno. Those 3 players were all eventually drafted in the top 12 of the NFL Draft. But that 2008 Georgia football team went 9-3. They fell far short of preseason expectations.

And what happened afterwards? Green and Moreno left school early. And Matthew Stafford, who later admitted he wanted to stay in school, was convinced to turn pro and leave. And the Georgia fans weren't heartbroken whatsoever. They were ready for Stafford to leave. Think about it. A future Super Bowl winning quarterback, and overall, #1 NFL Draft pick, and the Georgia fans were happy when he left. All the fans had heard was about how great this Stafford kid was, and he had never lived up to the hype. So why would anyone want to see another season of failed expectations? Stafford left, although he had originally told many he was staying.

In that same 2008 season, Kentucky football finished the regular season with a record of 6-6. And they even won a bowl game that season to finish 7-6. The Big Blue Nation wanted to have a parade and build statues! The difference in Georgia and Kentucky football in these seasons? Georgia had huge national championship hope. Kentucky was thrilled to go 6-6. Life is about expectations.

If you are going to venture into the world of Sports Gambling, one of the most important mindsets a gambler can have is that you aren't going to be the best. In fact, you probably aren't going to be very good at all, especially at the beginning. There will be gambling lessons and life lessons that you will learn along the way to make you better, but don't think that this is easy because you've watched sports all your life or played in high school. If it was that easy, there'd be a lot of winners out there.

BOTTOM LINE

Temper your expectations from the start of your sports gambling career. Go into it thinking that you will lose every penny of your initial bankroll (and you probably will). Yes, you can win at sports betting, but it's tough. And that doesn't mean you're a complete failure if you lose. A lot of smart people can't win at sports gambling. Good luck! You are going to need it. But keep your proper perspective: relationships are more important than cashing tickets. That's why this is nothing more than a **Side Hustle**.

6
REINVENTING YOURSELF:

Changing our actions and ways of thinking to become winners at sports betting and life.

"'Never say never because limits, like fears, are often just an illusion.' - Michael Jordan during his Basketball Hall of Fame Induction speech.

"The ceiling is the roof." - Michael Jordan during halftime of a North Carolina vs. Duke basketball game.

Okay, so maybe just one of these quotes makes complete sense. Even someone considered as good as anyone who has ever played the game can make mistakes. But this is further proof that "it's all about who you are in life." Michael Jordan says this and 20,000 people cheer. If a Square like you or I said this at a bar to a few people, we'd quickly be getting strange and dismissive looks as if we were ridiculous! By the way, I can admit that I was totally rooting for Patrick Ewing and Georgetown to beat North Carolina in the National Championship game pictured above that put Jordan on the map in the first place. And do you want to hear my conspiracy theory about Jordan having to retire in 1993 due to his gambling exploits? We will save that for the next book.

I can also admit this: Reinventing yourself is difficult and scary. A few years ago, basically on a whim, I decided to pursue a career in sports talk radio. Why would I do that in my 40's? I had no "ins" or connections to sports talk radio. I'd never played any sports. I wasn't related to anyone in the sports world. And none of my closest friends were into sports more than just being a fan. I was just a fan, but I was also trying to pick winners. What made me special enough to be given a chance? I approached it differently than everyone else who was attempting to do the same thing. I was not better, or not more talented, but different. While everyone else was trying to be biased fanboys of the local teams, I was trying to be unbiased and just pick winners against the point spread. That's what got me in the door: I thought and sounded differently than the others vying for the same goal.

Make sure to be different in what do you do in this world. Would you rather succeed on a small level copying everyone else? Or would you rather succeed on a much larger level doing things your own way and taking a risk. Sure, it's safer to do what everyone else does and just make it, but there will always be a ceiling to your success. Nothing ventured, nothing gained.

There is a very popular sports talk radio show in the state of Kentucky. Although the show revolves around one main host, the show has plenty of others to help the main host: multiple on-air co-hosts, producers, board-ops, people connected with the University of Kentucky athletics feeding the show information, callers lined up to vent their frustrations, etc. Marketing-wise, it's a great example of how to cultivate a product: placate a rabid sports fanbase and have a "Go Home Team" mantra every day. It works for them, and they reap the rewards. I give them full credit for the marketing aspect of their radio show, which is difficult now.

If I wanted to establish myself in sports talk radio in Lexington, Kentucky, all I had to do was sound exactly like the biggest radio show in the state. Easy money, right? It would seem easy, but it's not.

SIDE HUSTLE

I know that all kinds of people contact ESPN Radio in Lexington thinking they can start their own sports talk radio show and be a copycat of the fanboy shows. If I had tried to do that, I would have failed miserably. I honestly don't care who wins these games, as long as I'm on the right side against the point spread. I can bet on the local team one night, and bet against them the next night, without blinking an eye. The best sports gamblers in the world do that every single day.

How did I get into the sports talk radio world? By taking the following risks:

Find something that makes you stand out and original. All the good ideas in life are not taken. When I started my radio show based on sports gambling, it wasn't exactly greeted with open arms locally when I started.

There was a very well-known and respected member of the Lexington sports community that took me to lunch the first week I was with ESPN Radio in Lexington. As we sat at lunch, so many people walked up to him and said hello. I'm just sitting there like a loser while he was Mr. Popularity. Eventually, things settled down and he asked me what my "end game" was with ESPN Radio. I told him, and he didn't have much faith in anything I was saying. In fact, I remember him saying, "That will never work, and I wouldn't listen to you for 5 minutes." We then began a fierce debate about sports talk radio, what the good people of Lexington wanted to hear, and so on. After 2 hours, I don't think we settled anything. He made some good points, but I wasn't going to change at this point. I was already "pot committed" as they say in the poker world. This is what makes me different, and this is what I know about more than most, so here we go.

It took a while, but that guy who questioned me in the first week about my existence in the first place is now one of my biggest supporters. Well, at least he says he is. I don't know if I totally believe him. I know he also supports all the other shows on ESPN Radio in Lexington, but he swears I'm the only one he encourages! Bless his heart. Regardless, sometimes it takes a minute. But if you know you're doing the right thing, keep hustlin' until they tell you that you can't. And even then, keep going.

Don't be afraid to take chances. Risk takers can both win and lose big in life, but at least they step up to the plate. Would you rather go 0 for 4 with 4 strikeouts? Or just not play? At least the 0 for 4 guy gave himself a chance. I walked into the doors of ESPN Radio in Lexington proclaiming sports gambling was going to become legal soon, and I would put you ahead of the curve. They could have laughed me out of the room. My life was just fine before radio, and I would be just fine if they called security to remove me from the building. Taking chances, at any phase of life, can pay big dividends. And if one risk fails, that means you're closer to the next one succeeding. Whether you like Oprah Winfrey or not, she had 4 failed television shows that were canceled before she finally hit it big. And if it's good enough for Oprah, it's good enough for you. Because as we all know, it ain't Oprah till it's Oprah.

Run like hell with your idea. Make a new and fresh idea your own and go all in with it. And more than anything, own your idea. Until you are absolutely proven wrong or a money pit that can never be reversed, keep hustlin'. Nobody is going to help you more and better than you are.

Work your tail off. I truly enjoy doing my radio show, but I do that show alone. I have no producer, board-op, or nothing. And more importantly, I do all my own show prep. If there's a day that I'm not prepared, I can't just have a conversation with a co-host about the weather like others do or discuss our favorites fast food restaurants.

If I'm not ready every single day, I will bomb. It's just like sports gambling, if you don't find your work routine very day, you will bomb.

Perfect your craft every day. I do my radio show every day, including weekends, from Labor Day Weekend until the end of the NCAA Tournament on the first weekend in April. In the other months, I just do weekdays. But during the seasons, that's 8 solid months of working every day other than holidays and being pre-empted for live sporting events. In a college town/market, it's all about 3 sports in those 8 months: college basketball, college football, and the NFL. I try to listen to every show I do after it's over. I don't listen become I'm some narcissistic maniac who needs to hear himself, but I'm looking for mistakes. How can I do the show better? In sports gambling, we get better every day we handicap games. We learn what to do, and what not to do. What am I doing well, or not so well? We can even develop new systems with data-driven history that says it can make a profit. Every day of handicapping is a learning opportunity, and also experience to make you a better handicapper.

BOTTOM LINE

It's never too late to reinvent yourself in life and do something nobody else is doing. Whether you're bored with your career, or just want a change in life, change can be good! But we also can't throw complete caution to the wind and not realize the collateral damage of family implications. Getting into sports gambling is great, as long as others don't feel the wrath of the ups and downs that come with it. Make sure that isn't you when you reinvent yourself.

7
DAVID vs. GOLIATH

Mastering the Underdog Mentality

"Do you believe in miracles? Yes!" - Al Michaels calling the U.S.A. Olympic Hockey win over Russia in the 1980 Olympics.

Al Michaels is my favorite play-by-play announcer of all time. Not only was he great at his job, but he sometimes would sneak in a gambling reference when necessary. "That last score made this a very OVERwhelming game!" Unnoticed by many, but great for those of us who knew that the previous play put the game "over" the total. And in the early 1990's, I will swear to the bitter end that he made a call about San Diego Chargers running back Marion Butts, and Miami Dolphins linebackers Aubrey Beavers and Bryan Cox. It was something about Butts being surrounded by Cox and Beavers. Maybe that was wishful thinking, but I will keep searching YouTube for this potential all-time gem!

Anyway, the 1980 USA Hockey Team winning the gold medal in the Winter Olympics that year is recognized as possibly the biggest upset in the history of sports. But longtime oddsmaker Jimmy Vaccaro (we will hear more from him later) has said the odds on the USA to defeat Russia was 8/1 before they're matchup. We have seen much bigger upsets in sports history, but this is the Miracle On Ice! Disney made a movie about this team! They MUST be the biggest upset ever. It's a great story, but the numbers say it isn't. Sorry to burst their bubbles, but it's the truth.

But this was just a miracle. We should just take the favored teams all the time and everything will be fine. There's a reason why they're favored in the first place, right? If you believe that, then maybe sports gambling isn't for you.

Why do the favorites lose? This isn't something new! You've heard of David vs. Goliath? A story where a child named David took down the giant Goliath with 5 smooth stones. We glorify the biggest upset stories in history because they are so rare. We always root for David, but we bet on Goliath. But the point spread is the great equalizer because we overvalue Goliath in the desert. David always has more value!

It's too bad they actually play the games, instead of just playing them on paper. In the prehistoric days of college football (AKA up until the BCS started in 1998), there was no college football playoff or championship game. It was called the "mythical" national championship because the top teams rarely played each other. We really were just dreaming up matchups in our heads to see who the better teams were each year. It's crazy to think it wasn't that long ago when we lived in those days. Heck, college football had tie games until overtimes were created in the mid 90's.

Later in this book, we will go over the actual numbers proving how underdogs are a more profitable investment than favorites in every major sport. But the best teams are always vastly overrated. And when teams go on historic runs in the regular season, the media will often wax poetic in ridiculous fashion about those teams. The public eats it up and acts accordingly. And history tells us, it's usually wrong. Here are some obvious examples:

SIDE HUSTLE

In 2007, the New England Patriots almost went undefeated for the entire season. They went into the Super Bowl that year with an 18-0 record. All the pundits were crowning them as the greatest team of all time, BEFORE the Super Bowl. They were being compared to the undefeated 1972 Miami Dolphins at every turn. Of course, they lost the Super Bowl in the final minute. But that didn't stop people from betting on the Patriots as they were dominating the league. And the public lost their butts on them, too! Including the playoffs, the Patriots went 1-7 against the point spread in their final 8 games, and they lost all their last 5 games against the number. The public had believed the hype and jumped on the bandwagon with a huge favorite, and the public lost big.

The 2022 Los Angeles Dodgers were favorites to win the World Series, and rightly so! On August 13th of 2022, the Dodgers were 79-33 record, with a 17-game division lead. The Dodgers would end 2022 with the 4th most regular season wins in MLB history. Great time to get in on the money with this juggernaut right before the playoffs, right? Wrong again! Including the playoffs, the Dodgers "only" went 33-21 the rest of the way. But if you had bet $1 on the Dodgers every day after that 79-33 start, you would have lost $4.76 to the closing Money line (a –8.8% ROI). The public had made the Dodgers overpriced based on the recency bias and paid the price as a result.

In 2015, the University of Kentucky basketball team was loaded. They ran through all of college basketball in a dominating fashion all season, arriving at the Final Four with a 38-0 record. The media was constantly comparing them to the last undefeated team, the 1976 Indiana Hoosiers. But what the sports gambling world was missing, is that this Kentucky team was losing you money! When Kentucky lost their National Semifinal game to Wisconsin as a favorite, they had finished the NCAA Tournament with a 1-4 record against the spread.

In fact, this Kentucky team lost their bettors money over the entire season against the point spread.

In all these instances, teams that were being discussed as the best ever not only didn't finish the job, but cost the bettors a lot of money down the stretches of those seasons. Do underdogs win all the time? Of course, not. But the dogs usually have the value. And the more the media talks about favorites being unbeatable, those are exactly the times we should look to go against them.

BOTTOM LINE

There's a reason we still refer to David and Goliath. We love an underdog story. The problem is, we just don't like to bet on it. Historical data tells us that underdogs are more valuable than favorites over time. And the bigger and more dominant the favorite, the more valuable the underdog becomes. Look to take the dogs. They have more value long term than the favorites. By the way, is there some scroll somewhere that has the David vs. Goliath betting lines? And who took those bets?

SIDE HUSTLE

8
TAKING WHAT THE GAME GIVES YOU

How do us Squares find an advantage in sports betting?

"If you're not cheating, you're not trying!" - All my favorite professional wrestlers in the 1980's.

    Cheaters Always Prosper! Fantasy Football Index Magazine, the biggest selling fantasy football magazine on the market for decades, was looking for a columnist in 2000 to write about national fantasy football challenge contests. I was approached due to my modest success in national fantasy football contests. I wasn't looking to become a writer, but their tagline of "Cheaters Always Prosper" was what made me eventually say "yes." I'd been using that catch phrase all my life. It was like a sign from above! I'd been cheating all my life in silly little games that meant nothing. And now, I could be looked upon as a "Cheater" in the world of fantasy football. I enjoyed almost a decade with Fantasy Index Magazines back in the day.

    Like most kids of the 1980's, we learned all our life values from professional wrestling. But unlike most kids at the time, I always rooted for the bad guys! In those days, there was a clear line of Good vs. Evil. Since I knew from the very start that wrestling was "predetermined," and I knew it was a story. But not everyone in the 80's thought wrestling wasn't real. A mother of one of my friends in elementary school once told my mother that I was not invited back to their home, and I was to cut off all ties with her son. The reason? A bunch of us kids were watching wrestling, and I cheered when the bad guys won. And since she thought wrestling was real, she couldn't have a devilish criminal like me in her home or associated with her family. Upon hearing this, my mom had to hold back her anger and emotions, because nobody talked about her son like that, especially someone who thinks wrestling is real. As we got in my mom's car to drive away that day, my mother had a moment of clarity. "Don't you dare change who you are, son. It's okay to be different, especially around people like that. Don't ever lose your spirit." Occasionally, my mom threw her fastball with the best of them.

As a kid, I enjoyed watching professional wrestling. It was funny, and a male soap opera. I haven't watched since the 80's, but I had a list of my favorite professional wrestlers:

Randy "Macho Man" Savage – bad guy version only

1A. "Nature Boy" Ric Flair – bad guy version only

Anybody who went up against Hulk Hogan

I rooted for cheaters and the bad guys. That "take your vitamins and say your prayers" stuff that Hogan was saying was the worst! But in February 1988, I was going to try to make the WWE my **Side Hustle** for one night. NBC was going to show a prime-time edition of the WWE on a Friday night. To this day, it is still the highest rated wrestling program in television history. On that show, Hulk Hogan lost the WWE Championship to Andre the Giant, under very mysterious circumstances. Shocking, right? But the USA Today had a small blurb on Page 6 of their Entertainment Section (the Purple Section) that Friday morning almost in passing saying that Hogan had lost the belts on Thursday night in Indianapolis, and the edited version was going to be on national television that night. Sports gamblers read the USA Today back then, but they didn't read Page 6 of the Purple Section. Upon reading this, I immediately went around school to everyone I knew, trying to get action down on Andre defeating Hulk that evening. People thought I was ridiculous, but I had inside information those losers didn't. Of course, the following Monday every kid in school thought I had cheated them out of money, and I didn't get a dime from anyone. And that was fine, because I learned a lesson about having information that nobody else had, and how valuable it could be.

But in the real world, cheaters are everywhere. There's even a television show called *"Cheaters"* that just doesn't seem totally honest and truthful television. You know, like Maury DNA tests and lie detector tests honest and truthful television. It's easy to call anyone who has taken steroids or PED's a cheater. But who are the best sports cheaters of all time? In my lifetime, I have a top 3 of personal favorites:

Mike Scott, former MLB pitcher, Houston Astros. Scott was a mediocre pitcher in the early 80's from ages 24-29, going 29-44 with a 4.45 ERA. Then at age 30, he mysteriously/allegedly learned a new pitch called the split-fingered fastball from former MLB manager Roger Craig. Between ages 30-34, Scott went 86-49 with a 2.93 ERA, a Cy Young Award and a no-hitter. Wow! What an amazing turnaround so late in a pitcher's career to go from guy hanging on a major league roster to the best pitcher in MLB. Scott must have been a good student to learn a new pitch. Or did he just learn how to cheat? In the 1986 National League Championship Series, the New York Mets collected dozens of baseballs used in games pitched by Scott against them. All the baseballs had the same exact scuff marks in the same exact spots. What a coincidence! In 1987, Scott was accused scuffing baseballs by the San Francisco Giants. I have no idea why they would accuse him of anything! Scott only retired the last 26 batters he faced. That's nothing special! When approached by the umpires in the 9th inning of that game, Scott was clearly shown on television shoving things (plural) out of his glove and stuffing items down his shirt, and in his back pocket, as well as sliding something to his 2nd baseman, Bill Doran. Only his glove was searched, after he had already been caught on camera taking something out of his glove, and the game continued. The Giants went crazy, and rightly so. The players frantically asked the umpires to look in Scott's pocket and down his shirt, but the umps did nothing. The manager of those 1987 Giants? Roger Craig. They guy who allegedly taught Scott how to throw this mysterious pitch in the first place! He knew. Everybody knew! But Scott still got away with it. In 1986, Mike Scott said he would reveal whether he was cheating in a tell-all book to be released soon. Decades later, we are still waiting for that book.

Rosie Ruiz, "winner" of the 1980 Boston Marathon. Talk about someone who lived the gimmick until the bitter end! Ruiz ran the 1980 Boston Marathon in the 3rd fastest time in the history of the sport for a woman. Yet, no one saw her at any checkpoints throughout the race, and no one had ever heard of her. Ruiz started the race, got tired a couple of miles into the race, got on the subway, and emerged from the crowd a half mile from the finish. Tip to the wise: if you're cheating, don't win BIG. Just win under the radar. Don't try to win a million dollars counting cards at the casino, just try to win a few hundred and get out. In other words, try to remain unnoticed. Ruiz got back in the race too soon and finished too quickly. The woman was just trying to get an excused absence from her job, by using the race as what she was doing so she didn't have to work! As she crossed the finish line, she had no idea she was the first woman to cross, doing so with one of the fastest times for a woman in marathon history! In fact, you can see on her face that she didn't realize the mistake she had made until it was WAY too late. But once she was crowned the winner, she went all-in on her charade. When interviewed after the race, Ruiz didn't even know what simple race terms like "interval" or "split" meant. Other marathon runners have never seen her or heard of her before. And rightly so! She had never run a full marathon in her life! Not to mention, her legs weren't exactly those of a marathon runner, but more of a marathon watcher. But I give her credit! She passed away in 2019, but claimed until the day she died that she won that race. Living the gimmick until the bitter end for almost 40 years is admirable, even if she blatantly lied the entire time. By comparison, Pete Rose on whether he bet on baseball couldn't even last 15 years before he came clean.

Michael Larson, game show contestant, *Press Your Luck*, 1984. This is by far my favorite story of all-time in all sports or games. Larson was an out of work ice cream truck driver from Ohio who had to go to Goodwill to get a 50-cent shirt just to appear on Press Your Luck. Press Your Luck was a game show where the contestant took spins on a board and tried to win money, while avoiding the dreaded Whammy that took all your money. But Larson figured out that there was a pattern to the board, and he could avoid the Whammy every spin if he timed it correctly. Larson got a VCR, recorded every show, and memorized the patterns of the game board. If you're an out of work ice cream truck driver, what else are you going to do on a weekday morning? In theory, the average contestant was supposed to Whammy once every 6 spins. Larson went 45 spins in a row without hitting a Whammy. I remember watching these episodes as a kid on summer vacation, and they were completely mesmerizing. I'd never seen anything like it before or since. The crowd was going crazy, and the host was begging him to stop, but Larson kept his cool. Larson was celebrating split seconds after every spin, before anyone realized the result of the spin, because he KNEW he was taking CBS to the cleaners! He could have won a lot more money, but he stopped once he topped $100k. And this was 1984, so 100k then is a lot more now! CBS was so ashamed, they refused to let those episodes appear in any form of rerun for almost 20 years. It's on YouTube now, and it's incredible drama for a 1984 game show. CBS tried to get him for cheating after the show, but their lawyers gave them the honest truth: they couldn't prove that he had done anything wrong. He learned the patterns of the Whammy and beat the game. He did nothing wrong. CBS had to drop their charges and give Larson his well-deserved money.

The Larson story ends badly, because he thought he could live like that in the real world too. There's always been rumors of a movie being made of his life. Bill Murray and Nicolas Cage are stars that have been linked to a possible biopic, but it's never come to fruition. Heck, I would invest in a project like this, but I digress. Larson provided a valuable lesson to us sports gamblers, however. If the game gives us something, take full advantage of it. We don't get many opportunities in life to take the house. When we do, we must take absolute full advantage of it. And on this day in 1984, Michael Larson took the house. After Larson won big, CBS shut down the show until they got a whole new computer system with many different patterns. They wouldn't be cheated again, but they weren't cheated in the first place. They simply got outsmarted and outplayed.

What did all 3 of these people do? Did they break the rules? Yes and no. Did they know they were doing something shady? Of course, they did. But none of them truly got caught. Mike Scott never made the Hall of Fame, but you could argue he was the best pitcher in MLB for a 5-year period. By the way, Scott's home and road splits were incredible. He REALLY knew how to cheat at home in Houston! Rosie

SIDE HUSTLE

Ruiz never ran another marathon. Heck, she never ran the first one either. And Michael Larson asked CBS for a Press Your Luck Tournament of Champions, after he lost his money. CBS wasn't about to fall for that one. It doesn't end well for any of these alleged cheaters, but the theme is the same: take advantage of the advantage while it's there, because it doesn't last long.

That's great, **Side Hustle** Guy, but how do we get advantages over sports books like this? They're not going to fall for our silliness, and all those cheaters were from the prehistoric 1980's. Today, we must hustle for information. But in this day of internet and social media, it's very difficult to keep a secret in any major sport where millions of dollars are being wagered on each game. The books know what's happening before all of us squares know. That's one of many reasons why we are at a disadvantage before the games even start.

It's tougher to get a leg up on the sports books. And oddsmakers now have deals with leagues like MLB where they get each team's lineup, and can change the odds accordingly, before they are released to the public. That gives them the advantage over us. This is the biggest reason why I no longer bet NBA regular season games. It's so difficult to have other responsibilities in life and try to keep up with NBA lineup/load management decisions on a regular and timely basis. The NBA Playoffs are a much different story, but the regular season is just too much hustle for those of us who must get up every day and go to a career or help others who depend on us.

Legendary sports gambler Lem Banker tells the story of how he got word back in the 70's from that future Oakland Raider Hall of Famers quarterback Ken Stabler and wide receiver Fred Biletnikoff weren't going to start for the Raiders in their game against the San Diego Chargers that weekend. In fact, they weren't even going to travel with the team to San Diego for the game. How did Banker find this out? He got a phone call at 3:00 in the morning from a friend that knew Humm's father, who told him that his son was going to start for the Raiders. The Raiders were a huge 15-point favorite over the Chargers in this game, but this was under the assumption everyone for the Raiders played. Once the word got out to the Squares that Stabler and Biletnikoff were out, it was too late. The line had moved, and the Sharps had taken advantage. Of course, the game ended with a final score of 6-0, and the Raiders cashed the tickets. Money never sleeps, but you and I must get our sleep so we can go about our responsibilities the following day without feeling like death warmed over. That's why we are Squares and have to find other ways to grind out winners, and why the Sharps do things differently. And that's why we aren't Lem Banker, may he rest in peace. Some people would look at this as cheating, but it's not. It's taking what "the game" gives you.

But it's not just information that can help us take advantage of situations. As sports gambling spreads throughout the nation, sports books will offer deals to get new customers to sign up. If they are offering a percentage match up to a certain amount, take advantage of the full amount. For example, "Sports Book A will offer a 50% sign up bonus for an initial deposit of up to $1,000." Awesome! I will deposit $100 and get the bonus where it becomes $150. Why not deposit the full limit of $1,000 and get a $500 deposit?

And make sure to read the fine print in these bonuses! Many books will make you wager so much before you can cash out on these bonuses. Therefore, the "slow play" method works in betting 1-3% per wager like we do. One "all or nothing" bet might let you keep your bonus, but you could also lose your deposit and still not get your bonus if you don't hit the requirements. In other words, make sure you know the rules for each sports book when signing up, because they all have different rules and requirements to cash in on the gaudy sign-up bonuses they promise in huge font when you get started.

In my experience, it's better to get a cash bonus as a bonus rather than free plays. Again, read the fine print. Sometimes these free plays are one-time huge plays, or even required to play the bonuses in parlays.

And for sports gamblers that already have existing accounts, books will often give re-deposit bonuses as well. Here's another spot to take full advantage of any bonus the books offer. This is a long-term **Side Hustle**, not just trying to make a quick buck. Anytime a sports book gives you an advantage of any sort, you take it. It's too difficult to turn a profit to not do it.

BOTTOM LINE

This is a **Side Hustle** and we are Squares. We don't have inside information, and we don't have advantages. Other things come before handicapping games, so we must scour for our advantages where we can find them. For a new sports gambler just getting started, make sure to take full advantage of all the bonuses available. But also make sure to read the fine print and know what you truly must do to receive those bonuses, because sometimes the books can play a shell game and make you think you have more cash than you have. Take what the game gives you.

9
ACCOUNTABILITY

Knowing who you are and playing to your strengths in sports gambling.

"It ain't Keith Sweat's fault." - Brad Taylor, in a coming-of-age moment back in the day.

Often, other people can see things about you before you can yourself. This is why it's so important in this world to be self-aware. How quickly can you identify your strengths and weaknesses. For some sports gamblers, they never figure it out. But keeping track of your wagers and seeing what you're best at on paper or on your computer/phone screen, is an invaluable tool to becoming a successful sports gambler.

When I was a kid, I really enjoyed R&B music. I refer to it quite a bit in this book. I had several cassette tapes of popular artists from back in those days. And yes, I had cassette tapes because I didn't have a CD player for a long time. But for my money, Keith Sweat was the coolest cat in the yard. And if you see the picture of his album cover above, how can you not see it? In fact, I looked everywhere in Lexington, Kentucky for that sweater. I went to every Chess King and Merry-Go-Round I could find looking for it, and never found it. Everybody in Chess King and Merry-Go-Round stores back then were like me: they thought they were a lot cooler than they really were. In retrospect, I was probably lucky not to find it because of how lame that sweater looks today, but it crushed me at the time that I never found it.

In the late 80's, I thought I was cool. I was a total loser, but I didn't realize it at the time. The only solace was that I wasn't the only guy in that boat. In my opinion, all guys should have that yellow tape that says "police line – do not cross" around us until we reach 30 years old. We don't really "get it" until then, and some of us need a lot longer! But that didn't stop me! When I was trying to make the moves on the ladies back in the day, if you know what I'm saying (wink/wink, nudge/nudge), I would put on the Keith Sweat music and wait for the magic to happen. If anything could put a lady in the mood, it was Keith Sweat begging as only he could. If you remember his music, you know exactly what I'm talking about!

But if the ladies didn't fall for my charms, which I thought was impossible in the first place, the added Keith Sweat music wouldn't let me down. And if that failed to put them in the mood, I dismissed them as dumb. My misguided self-talk said it all! "If that chick didn't want any part of me, it was ONLY because she didn't like my Keith Sweat music. And since my music wasn't good enough for her, then she ain't good enough for me! She can step off (another 90's phrase)!" That's how delusional I was back in those days, driving home the fact that youth truly is wasted on the young!

After a little while, I started thinking that NO girl liked Keith Sweat music because every time I put on the cassette tape, the ladies would run for the hills. That can't be the case! His songs were on the radio all the time. Then I figured it out: it wasn't the great Keith Sweat. It was me! It's kind of like getting punched in the face. Eventually, if you get hit enough times, you learn to put your hands up and protect yourself. One day I looked in the mirror and finally realized, "it ain't Keith Sweat's fault." It's not like the ladies immediately begged to go out with me after this realization, but it helped to be a little bit more self-aware and knowing more about who I was and how others saw me. I had to change, not everyone else. It was another lesson learned.

This goes for sports gamblers as well. We have to be accountable for thinking that we are better handicappers than we really are. I know people who bet everything from UFC/MMA, Canadian Football League games, WNBA games, European Soccer games, and that's great! If someone can make money off all those sports, then more power to them! But it's okay to focus on 1 or 2 sports as a sports gambler. The best sports gamblers will tell you that they are only active in 1 or 2 sports. I focus on 4 sports year-round, but I could easily throw out a couple and possibly be an even better handicapper.

And this also goes for mistakes we make that are nobody's fault but our own. We all make mistakes. Whether it's sports gambling or real life, there are times when we make the wrong decisions. Often, we pay for them, both literally and figuratively. When I lose a sports wager based on picking the wrong team, I am not nearly as upset as you might think. I handicapped the game, made the choice, and lost. I will do the same thing tomorrow, and hopefully win.

One of the toughest things we deal with as sports gamblers is being accountable for our losing bets. The times when I get truly upset at myself are when I make my own mistakes. There are all kinds of slight errors that make me angry at myself:

Did I click on the wrong team when placing the bet?

Did I make a mistake in record keeping that made me take the wrong team?

Did I make a mistake on how much to wager?

Did I wait too long and get "shut out" by missing the start time?

Those are mistakes that upset me: errors that I can correct. Making bets that lose is not a mistake that I get upset about, because eventually it will come back to me.

However, it took a long time to get to that point. And it took a lot of life lessons to get there as well. When I first started, I'd get upset at losing. We all did. But getting to that point in your sports gambling career where one bet will never change your life is a coming-of-age moment.

One of the most important characteristics any of us can have in our lives is self-awareness. The ability to know who you are, and play to your strengths, not your weaknesses, can make the difference in not only sports gambling.

BOTTOM LINE

Be accountable for your own wagers in sports gambling. It's a decision you made, so stick with it. Know what sports your strengths are and play to them. As cliché' as it sounds, being a successful sports gambler is truly up to you. But if you're not winning, can you accept defeat and look in the mirror knowing that it's your fault? If you can, like I did decades ago about those mean ladies and my Keith Sweat mix tapes, you can get closer to that elusive profit in sports gambling.

SIDE HUSTLE

10
THE ULTIMATE LESSON

Bo Schembechler, Jeff Sagarin, and the 1989 NCAA Men's Basketball Tournament.

"A Michigan Man will coach Michigan!" - Bo Schembechler, hours before the 1989 NCAA Tournament.

You remember 1989, right? Madonna was pushing the envelope and cashing tickets on a shocked society, John Cusack was holding up his boom box, The Nintendo Game Boy kept kids occupied, Milli Vanilli was running an all-time **Side Hustle**, the Exxon Valdez spilled 11 million gallons of oil, and the movie cult classic *Roadhouse* got screwed out of many deserving Oscar awards. The Brad Wesley character in *Roadhouse* was a personal hero. The good old days, eh? The "good old days" weren't as exciting as we wax poetic about for us old people who endured it. There are only 2 good things about the good old days: they're over and we can learn from them.

In fact, there are only 3 things that were better in the 1980's and 90's than they are today: college basketball, music, and professional wrestling. That's it! That's the list! Everything else is better now, and I defy you to add or subtract from this list!

But growing up in Central Kentucky in the 1980's, I was inundated with college basketball. It was Kentucky Basketball 24/7, whether you liked it or not. If you didn't care for Kentucky basketball, like me, you were a troublemaker and a rabble rouser. You weren't one of us! I got that all the time, and still get it to this day! And when it wasn't college basketball, it was horse racing. College basketball and horse racing, as sports, aren't as popular as they used to be. But in the 80's, they still had a lot of cache' and popularity, especially in my neck of the woods.

And my couple of **Side Hustle** gigs as a kid revolved around these sports. One of them was going to a harness racing track called The Red Mile several times a week at night during the spring and summer months. I could run bets for other people, and I could place my own bets if I had the cash based on what these "experts" were telling me, using the term "experts" very loosely! In fact, I'd always try to fade these "experts" and not take the same horses they picked. It was so competitive that my dad didn't like it if I picked the same horse as he did, even if it won! That's a story I should save for my therapist. If the people I went to the track with finished the night in the black, that would make my life better cause I would get a little bonus at the end of the night for hustling and being a good sport. But I was a kid and had nothing better to do, so why not?

This story should tell you about my life as a kid. I went to a harness racing track in Lexington, Kentucky called The Red Mile a lot in the late 80's. My dad was always there when I went, because he loved to watch the horses. One Saturday night when I was in high school, I went to The Red Mile with my father. He did well that night, which was a rarity to say the least. And when he did well, that meant we ate like kings on the way home. This Saturday night, we stopped at a Shoney's Breakfast Bar at 11:00 at night. Nothing made me happier more than stuffing my belly (and my pockets) full of breakfast food that I could eat all night and even the next day! On this occasion,

SIDE HUSTLE

I saw some friends dressed to the nines at this breakfast bar: tuxedos, evening gowns, etc. I went up to them and spoke to them for a couple of minutes, shared some laughs, and discussed plans for later that evening (I was a borderline criminal at sneaking out of my parent's house late at night). When I rejoined my father, he asked me "Who are they?" And I told them they were friends from my school. The old man said "Well, they're awfully dressed up!" I said "yeah, it's Prom Night and they just came from there."

That was the moment my father lost all faith in me as a young man. He didn't have the same question I had for my friends, which was "how do you go to the Shoney's Breakfast Bar after leaving the prom?" Can't you go somewhere/anywhere else that might be a little classier? That escaped him. He looked at me with this look of amazement that his only son would be one of those losers that didn't even go to his high school prom. It's not like I was breaking the hearts of every teenage girl in Central Kentucky, either. But I then explained to him that he should be proud of me, instead of ashamed. Not only had I saved money by not going, but I made money at the horse track. I had my eyes on the big picture, because I was moving to Atlanta soon and needed to save all the money I could. While all my school friends might have those "wonderful" Prom Night memories to last a lifetime, I had a few extra dollars in my pocket that would help my goal of leaving Kentucky for Atlanta. So many people talk about memories, experiences, and "the best things in life are free"-type phrases, which I understand completely. But I was always a "big picture/big topic" kind of guy. Whether it's sports talk radio today, or trying to hustle as a kid, I was always about The **Bottom Line**. While to my people, not going to my high school prom made me "weird," a "loser," and all the insults you would expect being thrown at a kid that chose going to a horse track over going to the prom, I didn't care.

SIDE HUSTLE

I was preparing for the future, and subconsciously practicing for the world we live in today. Later that night, there were plenty of friends who told me that they were truly jealous of the fact I went to the track instead of going to the prom. Just don't tell my people that I had to sneak out of the house in the middle of the night to find out!

Running bets at The Red Mile was one of my **Side Hustle** gigs in 1989. The other was NCAA Tournament bracket pools. The first time I did a bracket pool was in 1981. I was in elementary school, years away from becoming a teenager. But in terms of sports knowledge, I was quite a bit ahead of my peers at a young age. In fact, I had a college basketball preseason magazine that I took to school in elementary school one time to occupy my mind during the constant down times of boredom to try to stay out of trouble. The magazine had the Top 20 teams for the upcoming season ranked in order 1 to 20 on the cover. The kid sitting next to me asked to see the magazine, and I gave it to him. It was weird because he NEVER talked to me. He looked at the list of Top 20 teams, and San Francisco was ranked #20. For those of you of a certain age, those were the Quintin Dailey years. It's scary that I remember that. But anyway, the kid sees San Francisco ranked as the #20 team in college basketball and assumes that they're the worst team. He starts singing this song "San Franciscoooooo" in a very sad, pathetic voice as if they were a cartoon character who had an anvil fall on him from out of nowhere. As I tried to explain to him that #20 in college basketball doesn't mean they're the worst, it means they're very good, he kept singing that silly song. He was having too much fun sounding pitiful, and it was very funny! At that point I said to myself "Screw it! Just play along. This kid has never said a word to me, and now he's singing!" We sang that song for months, for no reason. Every time something bad happened to someone in class, we would sing "San Franciscoooooo" and laugh hysterically, all because he thought being ranked #20 was the worst team in college basketball. Ironically, that kid and I kind of lost touch as we went through school, as we didn't run in the same circles. It wasn't anyone's fault. It's just life. But when we graduated high school, we did see a spot where we ran across each other and said hello for the first time in several years. The first thing he said was "Remember when we thought San Francisco was the worst team? We were so dumb!" I just went along with it. "Yeah, we were dumb." We hugged each other and went our separate ways. But I never forgot that because if I had corrected him and been a buzzkill, neither of us would remember that time. Patience and growing relationships regardless of the situation are good qualities, both in sports gambling and in real life, regardless of age.

And if you think being a sports gambler is a learned trait, and something you aren't born with, I have Exhibit A to argue that. In 1981, I needed Indiana to defeat North Carolina in the championship game to take home some money in a bracket pool and some old general store out in the country. Yes, it's as "down home" as it sounds, and as you can imagine. On the day of that championship game, President Ronald Reagan was shot. He ended up being fine, but it was a scary moment in history. Back then we only had 4 channels on TV, so it was on every channel. Being a kid in elementary school, and knowing everything was going to be okay, it really didn't bother me a whole lot......UNTIL someone on TV in passing mentioned they might cancel the NCAA Championship Game between Indiana and North Carolina that evening. NO! Don't cancel that game! If they did, I wouldn't win my bracket pool, and I wouldn't get any money. And at that time, it was more about the "prestige" of winning a bracket pool against all my dad's friends than to win the money.

President Reagan healed up nicely, the championship game was played on schedule, Indiana won, and I got to cash my first ticket in a bracket pool in 1981. My dad came home and gave me a few $1 bills and said the rest was a "finder's fee." I didn't care! My family gave me everything I wanted anyway. I was a little kid walking around knowing he was smarter than everyone else cause he picked the games correctly, and you couldn't put a price on that. So, I took my $1 bills, went to my room, and started playing Atari until it was time to go back to school the next day. But the fact that I cared more about a basketball game not being canceled rather than the health of the POTUS should have been a sign of things to come.

Winning can be the worst thing for a beginner, because then you think you are good. But to be honest, you're just lucky. There's a reason why "Beginner's Luck" is a term we've all heard before. Sometimes that isn't the case, but most of the time it is. In my mind, of course I was a genius! Starting in 1982, I started watching a ton of college basketball so I could be ready for those brackets in March. We lived so far away from everything that we couldn't even get cable television. Thankfully, my parents got one of those old "radar" satellite dishes that sat out in the yard and was nothing but a huge eye sore. But I could watch basically anything I wanted to watch. Use your imagination for answers to what teenage boys with the ability to watch absolutely anything on television joke here! It was baseball. Yeah, baseball...

Anyway, like most sports gamblers that experience early success, the winning went to my head as well. I thought I was now Mr. College Basketball! I watched every game on ESPN during the week, and on the local and national networks on the weekends. Unlike now, when national networks can't draw flies for college basketball regular season games, they felt like events when I was a kid. Being in SEC country, we were inundated with SEC Basketball throughout January and February. Tom Hammond and the late Joe Dean Sr., the announcers for SEC Basketball when I was a kid, seemed to be everywhere! They would make a Wednesday night game in Oxford, Mississippi with less than 5,000 in attendance feel like a sellout at Madison Square Garden. I remember on some Saturday's those guys would broadcast a game in the afternoon, travel to another town, and broadcast another SEC game that evening! And I watched every one of them, mainly because I was growing up on a farm in the middle of nowhere during a long, cold winter and had nothing else to do and no friends close by to pester. But also, I thought I was sharpening up for the NCAA Tournament bracket pools in March since I was now the self-proclaimed Mr. College Basketball.

But a funny thing happened in those years after early bracket pool success, and concentrating more on the sport for which I was allegedly the smartest guy in the room. I couldn't pick the games correctly anymore. From trying to outsmart people, to getting cute, to having an ego, to simply regressing to the mean, suddenly all those people I thought were dummies when I defeated them rubbed it in my face when they defeated me. And despite not realizing at the time how difficult winning at sports gambling was, it was very humbling. That didn't sit very well with me whatsoever. Or as Michael Jordan said at every turn in *The Last Dance*, "I took that personally."

But it just continued to get worse! In 1985, the NCAA Tournament Final Four was played in Lexington, near my home. This was it! Finally, I was going to cash in bracket pools again and get just a little dignity back. We got to the finals and all I needed was Georgetown to defeat Villanova in the Championship Game. Easy money! Georgetown was a 9.5-point favorite in that game, and the USA Today headline read "Villanova vs. God." And Georgetown had already defeated Villanova twice in the regular season. Feels like a win to me. Of course, they played the game and Villanova defeated

SIDE HUSTLE

Georgetown, playing an almost perfect game to do so. And for a kid who put everything into the brackets every year, it was devastating. I couldn't deal with losing anymore. I had nothing else going on in those days, so it just stews in your mind for a while. Like today, some people will remember a "Bad Beat" for a very long time. We don't remember the wins as much as we remember the losses! And there's nothing worse in life than thinking you are the smartest guy in the room, and you're far from it. That was me at that time, and it was embarrassing.

After that, I tried to do what The Good Book tells us and put away my childish things. No more brackets! Let's try studying and getting into a prestigious college or something boring like that. But come 1986, I didn't pay attention to college basketball anymore nearly like I had in the past. I was going to focus on school topics that I didn't like, girls who wouldn't give me the time of day, getting a driver's license so I could escape the farm, and getting a **Side Hustle** to make some cash. Easy life, huh? But just like in *The Godfather*, just when I thought I was out, they pulled me back in.

My mother, bless her heart, could tell I was depressed. So, when the basketball tournament was drawing near, she offered to let me stay out of school for the first 2 days of the NCAA Tournament so I could stay home and watch them on television instead of having to go to school and be miserable. Well, that's awfully nice of her. Being a public-school teacher herself, she could tell a couple days off like that would be beneficial to someone like me, who was seemingly just going through the motions at the time. I took her up on her offer, and the wheels started to turn. Just like that, I was back into The Bracket Game. My mother had no idea that she had recreated a monster.

In fact, since I was going to get a couple days off from school thanks to my mom, there was no reason not to try to make my own

SIDE HUSTLE

Side Hustle from this newfound opportunity. Let's start OUR OWN Bracket Pool. And before you know it, I'm handing out brackets to every kid I knew in school. You can play for $1, or $5 for the high rollers (AKA faculty). This wasn't the same **Side Hustle** as a friend of mine who had a Ziploc back full of folded up pieces of paper. For 50 cents each, some unsuspecting Square can draw one of those teams out of the bag to win big cash prizes. The trick was that the folded papers were only the 15 and 16-seeded teams. I knew what he was doing, and we just laughed. He said he wouldn't rat on me, if I didn't rat on him. But the thing was, I was a legitimate "businessman" at the time! I wasn't hustling anyone, unless you count that 25-cent fee per dollar of entry fee for bracket pool entries. Quarters were like gold in high school at the time because we didn't have machines that could take ATM cards or even give change for $1 bills. He who had the most quarters won in those days.

But I started running a bracket pool in high school. I did it right, and I took the days off from school that my mother gave me to run them and count the results. Each year, the bracket pool got bigger and bigger. And I kept making more and more money. One year, I was called to the front office just as school began on the day before the Tournament started. Of course, like an 80's sitcom when teenagers would kiss for the first time, all the other kids in the audience would yell "woooooooh" to make me feel like a criminal. On my way out the door, the male teacher – WHO HAD MULTIPLE ENTRIES IN MY BRACKET POOLS – asked me not to mention his name if I was getting busted for running bracket pools. I looked at him like he was the biggest loser ever and agreed to not rat him out. Not only was this guy a Square, but a chicken bleep as well. Thanks for all your help, sir! I might be going to Detention for the rest of the school year, but I'll save your scaredy cat butt out of loyalty, sir! Unbelievable!

SIDE HUSTLE

Upon arriving in the school official's office, I was asked what I was doing. I said I didn't know what he was talking about. I wasn't falling for that trick. Then the school official tried every way in the world to get me to admit I'm running this horrible bracket pool that was just the worst thing ever. Every time he asked, I had the same response: "I don't know what you're talking about, sir." I'm a teacher's kid, with ice water in my veins when it comes to anything school related. I knew what I could get away with, and what I couldn't. This made me extremely dangerous in the eyes of most teachers, and they were correct! Any reference to something being put on your "permanent record" was an often-used threat in those days that held absolutely no substance. Where is this permanent record today? It's like Bigfoot. Show me the body of a dead Bigfoot and I'll believe it exists. It amazed me how many kids fell for the "permanent record" stuff, but I digress.

But after we danced around for a couple minutes, the school official knew I wasn't budging. He had to make the first move, or else we weren't going to get anywhere. What did I care? I wasn't sitting in class! Finally, he reached into his pocket, slammed a $10 bill on the table, and said "Cut the crap, Taylor. I want in your bracket pool!" He slid the money to me. Then, and ONLY after I had my grubby hands on his money, did I act as if I had a light bulb appear over my head. If he was still going to bust me, he wouldn't have gotten his $10 back. "Ooooh, you mean the bracket pool?" I reached in my backpack that I just happened to have with me for some odd reason, and gave him a couple of blank bracket sheets, and said "please have these back to me by 3:00 this afternoon because I think I'm coming down with the sniffles and probably won't be at school Thursday or Friday, sir. That's just a hunch." He then said "Oh no, Taylor! You're going to sit here and help me fill these out!" It's very telling when someone in power always refers to you by your last name, and never your first, but I digress. We went ahead to talk about college basketball, and other stuff for most of the first hour of school. I didn't care because I just didn't want to go back to class and that snitch teacher who wanted me to protect his pristine name if I'd been busted.

I walked back into class, and the teacher's eyes went WIDE open desperately asking me what happened. I'd been gone for almost an hour and the guy was sweating! All I did was shake my head "no," while not saying a word. Suddenly, this man starts yelling at me like I had burned his house down, telling me how I'VE just ruined his career and I hope I can live with myself. I just stood there, no facial expression changes whatsoever, taking his verbal abuse, in front of the entire class as they sat silently in shock. I knew he was humiliating himself, and just let him do it. After he was done, I told him "Sir, the school official simply wanted to enter my bracket pool and told me how proud he was of me for being such an enterpriser while offering a much-needed service for the moral of faculty and students." At that moment, the bell rang, and everyone left the classroom in laughter as the teacher looked like a real jerk. We never discussed this matter again, and I received A's in his class the rest of the year while doing even less work than I had previously. Amazing how that worked out, huh?

Neither the school official nor my self-centered wimp of a teacher cashed their brackets, thankfully. But it's ironic that sports gambling can have bracket pool standings sheets with names of the most powerful and popular of faculty members, and the lowest of snot-nosed first-year students next to each other. It also taught me a valuable lesson that I have kept with me to this day: no matter who you are, sports gambling can make anyone (and everyone) do things they wouldn't normally do, both positive and negative.

SIDE HUSTLE

But back in 1986, I had given up on bracket pools. I stopped religiously following the sport of college basketball and was tired of donating money to the local bracket pools that I thought were won by morons. When my mom let me stay home from school to watch the first two days of the NCAA Tournament, I got back in. But who do I pick? I don't know as much about the sport as I did before.

In the 80's, the USA Today Newspaper was the first internet. America Online came in the 90's, but information-wise it was just USA Today on your computer screen! I loved USA Today so much that I asked my parents for a subscription as a Christmas gift. My mom was truly very upset when she told me that we lived too far out in the middle of nowhere for them to deliver it. That just fueled the fire to get off the farm as soon as I could, but I digress.

On the Monday before the NCAA Tournament, USA Today had a special section full of all the information anyone would need to know about it. There were several pages on all the information you could think of, but the best information was on the very last page. It's almost like they were hiding it from the Sharps so that the Squares would be distracted by all the pomp and circumstance. In one corner, the odds from Las Vegas were printed. And in the other corner, someone named Jeff Sagarin had his computer ratings. Sagarin graduated from MIT in 1970, and still posts his sports computer ratings to this day. He's a personal hero, based on the NCAA Tournament alone. Since I had been losing every year since 1981, I decided that I wasn't going to put myself through the torture of second guessing myself for 11 months again. I would go ahead to fill out 2 brackets: one based on the odds in the desert, and one based on Jeff Sagarin's ratings. In other words, take all the guesswork out of things, and let the numbers speak for themselves. If I lose, it's on them, and not me.

SIDE HUSTLE

Immediately, I started winning. In 1986, a combination of Duke and Louisville would make the finals. In 1987, Indiana won it all. And in 1988, nobody had Kansas winning it, but the numbers were so good on the rest of the teams that it cashed again. 3 years of tournaments, and 3 years of cashing tickets in bracket pools. Easy money, right? This will never end!

But in 1989, the ultimate lesson in sports handicapping was about to be given. Going into the NCAA Tournament, Las Vegas had Georgetown and Arizona as co-favorites to win the national championship, but neither team made the Final Four. As the Tournament began, the USA Today's special Tournament Edition printed Jeff Sagarin's ratings as usual, and Sagarin had Michigan winning it all. Michigan? Wait a minute! Check those ratings again! Michigan basketball in 1989 was several years pre-Fab Five, but they had plenty of NBA talent. In fact, 6 members of the 1989 Michigan Basketball team would eventually play in the NBA. But you wouldn't know that by how the team played that regular season.

The 1989 Michigan Basketball team was good, but far from great, in the regular season. They finished with a 24-7 record, and 3rd in the Big Ten Conference. In the last game of the regular season, Michigan lost to Illinois by 16 points at home, on CBS national television. I remember seeing the final score of that game and thinking, "Michigan has no chance to win it all." It was the 2nd time Michigan had lost to Illinois that season, and both times they lost by double digits. Heck, they had lost to Alaska-Anchorage in Utah during a holiday tournament! And not only that, but Michigan's recent NCAA Tournament history didn't make anyone feel confident at all. In 1985, Michigan was a #1 seed and lost in the 2nd round to eventual national champion Villanova. And yes, Villanova went on to beat a much

SIDE HUSTLE

better team in Georgetown. There was no pedigree for success here, unless you listened to Jeff Sagarin.

Michigan entered the 1989 NCAA Tournament as a 3-seed. That itself raised some eyebrows, mainly because of how they were humiliated at home in their final regular-season game. But things were about to get even fuzzier less than 48 hours before the NCAA Tournament started. Bill Frieder, the Michigan head coach, announced that he was resigning from his job at Michigan and taking the same job at Arizona State. But he would go AFTER the NCAA Tournament and continue to coach his current team until they were eliminated from the Tournament. Fair enough.

No, it wasn't! Bo Schembechler, at that time the Athletic Director of Michigan, would have none of that foolishness. Schembechler was about as bitter of a man as one can imagine whether you were a Michigan fan or not. "A Michigan man will coach Michigan, not an Arizona State man," yelled a battle-toughened Schembechler, who fits our "bitter to the end" characteristic of a sports figure that we love in sports talk radio. So Frieder was out, some previously unknown guy named Steve Fisher was the interim coach for the Tournament only, and Michigan would find a new coach in the offseason.

So, Michigan basketball was in a state of turmoil mere hours before the NCAA Tournament was to begin. But according to Jeff Sagarin, off court issues are not considered. In fact, Sagarin's ratings had Michigan rated #1 going into the Tournament. Okay, Sagarin. Are you on to my little **Side Hustle** here? There's no way anyone is going to predict Michigan to win the 1989 NCAA Tournament when they JUST FIRED THEIR COACH in the same week! This created a true dilemma for me. Do I use conventional wisdom, think for myself, and ignore the Sagarin ratings to go against Michigan? Or do I blindly believe in these numbers that have been so financially good for me in the last few years? And since I never told anyone how I picked these games so successfully, I had no one to bounce stuff like this off to get a sane opinion other than mine. I had to keep the secret alive!

In situations like these, I often asked my mom coded questions to help make decisions in my life. This time, I asked her the following: "Mom, if you had an important decision to make, would you trust numbers? Or yourself?" She replied, "Do what works best for you and makes you different and better than anyone else." Good enough for me! I'm not sure how often she followed that advice, but it worked for me. The old "do as I say, not as I do" mentality, I suppose. With that in mind, I put Michigan winning the national championship on my bracket. I gave my dad my bracket for him to send in places I couldn't. My dad looked at the bracket with Michigan winning it all, and he just laughed and threw my paper on the ground. "Boy, you better have your own entry fees cause I ain't having my name or money associated with this crap." He didn't use the word "crap." I gave him the money. He still called me all sorts of names, but I made him swear to give my brackets in the same places he did. He finally said he would, saying "It's your money, boy."

The NCAA Tournament plays out, and Michigan wins their first 2 games by very close margins against inferior teams to make the Sweet 16 round. Ironically, Michigan would play North Carolina in the Sweet 16 round in Lexington! I had a friend who is a big North Carolina fan, for some reason, and we both went to the game. Michigan was the underdog in the game but won going away. My friend was pissed, and I was ecstatic. My trust in the numbers was paying off. My friend had tickets for the Elite 8 round game too, but he didn't want to go because his team had lost. The only trick was, he told me this an hour before the game started when I stopped by his house to pick him up. 1989 was not the time of cell phones or social media. I didn't have access to a mobile phone, so I couldn't just text someone to go at a moment's notice. Time for another quick-thinking **Side Hustle**: sell the extra ticket! And if I must drive to the arena to sell the ticket at short notice, then I'm going to sit there and watch the game too. So, I sold the extra ticket and watched the game myself. That might be the only sporting event I ever attended by myself, but this was a special occasion. This was my victory lap. It's me bragging to myself about what a great decision I made following the numbers, and not conventional wisdom. Michigan defeated Virginia by 37 points that day to make the Final Four. I looked like a genius for doing one thing: trusting in the data.

Georgetown and Arizona were the favorites to win the 1989 NCAA Tournament, but Illinois probably should have been. They ended the season 31-5, Big Ten Champions, and a #1 seed themselves featuring 5 future NBA players on their roster. All I needed was Michigan to defeat Illinois in the National Semifinals, and I was a big winner once again. Anyone still alive in bracket pools had Illinois winning it all. But by this time, even the desert had jumped all over the Michigan bandwagon. Illinois was the #1 seed, Michigan the #3 seed. Illinois had defeated Michigan TWICE during the regular season by double digits! And don't forget, Michigan was playing with a head coach who had only coached 4 games in his entire 2-week career! And Illinois was only a 1.5-point favorite in the Final Four over Michigan? The desert was telling us something in that line: Michigan was the better team, being such a short underdog under these circumstances.

This Final Four game was played on a Saturday night, but I was going to stay home and watch it for 2 reasons: I had a lot of money on the line, and I did not want to be seen in public acting like a moron regardless of the outcome. At home, I would be calm because my parents would have made sure I behaved! The game was close all the way, and Michigan won at the end. For my purposes Michigan defeating fellow #3 seed Seton Hall in the Championship was almost irrelevant because I had already cashed in on Michigan simply making the finals and nobody else in their right minds had Michigan or Seton Hall winning it all. The job was complete.

I remember going out after that Michigan-Illinois game with quiet confidence I rarely had up to that point in my life. I had taken a chance on the numbers, and won big, when everyone (including my own dad) thought I was ridiculous. Yet another Private Victory, which we will discuss later, that I was only able to celebrate on my own. And I have kept that lesson with me to this day. When my mom gave me those winnings in 1989, I thanked her, hugged her, and kissed her on the cheek, because one comment she unknowingly made in passing gave me the courage to take a chance I may not have taken on my own. Showing my mother love like that was something I rarely did in those days because I was a teenager who needed to grow up. I have grown up now, but winning is the deodorant that covers all the stink.

According to our friends at SportsOddsHistory.com, Michigan has 12/1 odds of winning the national championship pre-Tournament in 1989. They would become the longest shot to win the Tournament for another 8 years until Arizona defeated three #1 seeds to win the Tournament in 1997. And as of the 2024 Tournament, only 6 teams with bigger odds have won the Tournament in the 34 years since Michigan cut down the nets in 1989.

The 1989 Michigan Wolverines men's basketball team will always be one of my favorites. It taught me the most valuable lesson in sport handicapping. Eye tests and gut feelings are one thing, but numbers and data are another. To this day, the most valuable lesson

I've learned in sports handicapping is to bet numbers and data, not teams and people.

What else did I learn from all of this? *Trust the Process* is a slogan used by fans of the NBA's Philadelphia 76ers, though it has since become popular elsewhere in sports and culture. Coined during a rough patch for the team, it basically means "things may look bad now, but we have a plan in place to make it better." But it can apply to our everyday lives, too. Sometimes we have doubts in ourselves, and it can come in all phases of life: sports gambling, career, relationships. The list is endless. And the times when we have doubts about what we do well are the times we often live to regret. Sports gambling involves a lot of trust in yourself. And yes, it's difficult to have a lot of faith when you have lost every night for 2 weeks. But it happens to all of us! You aren't too good for a long losing streak, and neither am I. A sick way of looking at it can be classifying it as The Joy of Pain. I know too many sports gamblers who don't have faith in what they are doing, and they will take some time off when a cold streak hits.

You don't know as much as the numbers do. But don't take that personally! The oddsmakers in the desert don't know as much as the numbers either! They are just smart enough to rely on them much more than the normal sports gambler. It's in the sports gambler's best interest to use a data-based handicapping process when trying to pick winners.

Can this still work today? Sure! You'd be amazed at how many people still use their "gut instincts" and self-validated "eye tests" to pick brackets. Following the Vegas odds and Sagarin ratings (and of course, our newest college basketball hero Ken Pomeroy, whom we will discuss later) are still safe and potentially profitable bets when filling out brackets, but they do not always win. My mom started to panic when we didn't cash in for a while during the 1990's. I informed her that if there are 50 people with 1 entry in a bracket pool, in theory, one person should only win once every 50 years. She finally got it. I think she did alright.

BOTTOM LINE

Today, we handicap games and tournaments much differently than using just odds in the desert and Jeff Sagarin ratings. But the principle remains the same: trust the numbers and data more than you trust yourself when handicapping sports. Relying on "hunches" and liking "the cut of someone's jib" isn't a reliable way to handicap sports long term. As sports handicappers, we should also be as unbiased as possible. Swallowing your pride and believing in the data will make you a better handicapper.

SIDE HUSTLE

11
DELUSION

The Chris Moneymaker/William Hung Effect

"She Bangs!" - *William Hung.*

Remember back in olden times? You know, the decade of the 2000's? There were 2 very prominent people who made their debuts in that time, both of whom took full advantage of their moment of fame. The sad thing is that so many people saw them, they drove thousands of others to failure.

The Moneymaker Effect was a real thing. In 2003, a kid named Chris Moneymaker who was an accountant in his 20's in Knoxville, Tennessee, played in an online poker tournament for $86. He parlayed that into $2.5 million by winning the World Series of Poker (WSOP). His timing was perfect, as ESPN was televising the WSOP for the first time with cameras to show cards that the players were holding. Moneymaker was a nobody at the time, but that was about to change. Moneymaker took down some of the biggest names in poker with strong play and amazing bluffs. The old guard of poker Sharps could not figure out this Square. Moneymaker played brilliantly, and deserved every penny, but we didn't know what was about to happen.

SIDE HUSTLE

After Moneymaker won the WSOP, the Poker Boom took place immediately. Every guy who played poker every Saturday night in the basement with his friends now had hope that they could do the same thing Moneymaker did. The internet was flying with new poker players playing 18 hours a day, and the migration to Las Vegas was on. Chris Moneymaker changed the game, and changed the world, with one nationally televised tournament run. Thousands of new poker players were in the WSOP by the next year, and *The Moneymaker Effect* was on. And all this pomp and circumstance gave a lot of people the fever! Countless droves of poker players headed out to the desert to go all in on becoming a poker superstar like Chris Moneymaker. For most, it did not happen.

In 2004, William Hung was a student at Cal-Berkeley. It was also the 3rd season of American Idol, which was the biggest show on television for the entire decade of the 2000's. The star of the show was Judge Simon Cowell. He was a master of insulting those contestants who wasted his time, and the viewers loved it. A modern-day Howard Cosell, who told it like it was.

Hung performed his now infamous rendition of *"She Bangs"* by Ricky Martin. After this comedy gold, Cowell told Hung, "It's one of the worst auditions we have this season. Everything about it was grotesque. You can't sing! You can't dance! So, what do you want me to say? Go and do your homework!" Cruel? Yes. Good television? Yes. Hung replied, "I have no professional training." To which Cowell sarcastically replied, "No! There's the surprise of the century!"

But the American public would not let this die! Hung's performance was so terrible but memorable, that he became a cult hero and appeared on several talk shows of the day. Hung then released his own album, selling over 200,000 copies. Hung also released a holiday album that only sold 35,000 copies. But the damage

SIDE HUSTLE

was done. Hung made the most of his 15 seconds of fame. But this was great for American Idol as well. Now, thousands of people were looking to simply audition for the show and getting paid like Hung got paid.

Moneymaker and Hung both had amazing moments in time. Unfortunately for them, they have never come remotely close to replicating their brief successes. Moneymaker still plays poker, but in the over 2 decades since his WSOP win, he hasn't won prize money combined in those decades that match his 1 paycheck in the 2003 WSOP. Hung "retired" from music in 2011 and is a motivational speaker still cashing in off his fame. Do not knock their **Side Hustle**!

The lesson from this is that just because Squares like Moneymaker and Hung had success does not mean that everyone else can. Is there anything more painful (and entertaining) to see delusional performers on American Idol think that they're great, but are awful? And there is nothing the poker Sharps love more than to see a Square at their table trying to be the next Moneymaker.

The same goes for sports gambling. How many people moved to the desert thinking they can bet on sports for a living? Many! How many people succeeded? Few. I keep trying to yell from the mountaintops that sports gambling is extremely difficult. If you get into this, you're not going to be the next Moneymaker of poker or Hung of, well, whatever it was that Hung did.

Delusion is a very cruel emotion. It's the biggest liar in the world. It tells you that you can do something when you can't. We are always told to shoot for your dreams. I get it. But there is also a limit! I'd like to be POTUS, but that ain't happening.

Delusion is a terrible thing to possess, especially when you don't realize you have it. In my world of sports talk radio, I see it all the time. EVERYONE thinks sports talk radio is easy. All you have to do is watch ESPN SportsCenter, roll off the couch, and start talking. Easy money, right? And especially in my world of sports gambling, there is no way I can just roll off the couch and start talking. I do a show by myself. I MUST be prepared. If I'm not prepared, I'll just sit there and talk about the weather. I say quite often that "my show might stink, but at least I'm prepared to stink."

I get that in sports talk radio all the time as well. People tell me all the time that I'm great on the radio. But be honest with yourself: do you actually think a friend of yours would come up to you and say "wow, you are terrible on the radio. How do you still have a job?" I'm told constantly by people I know that I'm great on the radio. But friends aren't going to tell you that you're terrible, even if it's obvious that you are. My mom tells me I'm the best radio host ever. Then I remind her that she's my mom and she's biased. Although that still doesn't shut her up, she gets the point.

Do you think you can hit 52.38%? Maybe you can. Do you think you can hit 70%? Not a chance. Sure, you can go 7 out of 10. You could go 35 out of 50 for a stretch. But if you are like us, going 361 days a year, you aren't hitting 70%. In fact, if you hit 53% for a calendar year, you should be shopping for a yacht. Per 1,000 plays, the odds of a sports bettor hitting 70% of their bets are 1 billion to one. Are those the odds you think you can defy? If so, your expectations need to be checked, and rechecked. Sorry, you can't hit 70%.

BOTTOM LINE

Chris Moneymaker and William Hung are names that are still well-remembered over 20 years after their initial hits. That's the good news. The bad news is they had many copycats who could not pull off the same miracle. 60% winning sports wagers is not going to happen for you, but 53% winners can. Don't try to be the next Moneymaker or Hung. Make your own way in sports gambling, doing it your way.

12
STAYING THE COURSE

Dealing with losing

"It doesn't matter if the horses are blind, just load the wagons." - John Madden.

Madden said he told his Raiders teams this before every game, and nobody knew what he was talking about. Madden even said he had no idea what it really meant, but it worked. Maybe it worked because he had a roster filled with future Hall of Famers? Yeah, that helped tremendously. The Vanderbilt football coach can say the same exact thing to his team before every game, but they aren't going to go out and beat Alabama to win the SEC Championship. Eventually, the game is played on the field or court, not with words in the locker room or in the media.

But as sports gamblers, we can take some solace in this quote. And my interpretation of this is that things aren't always going to go well. We will face times when it doesn't look like we will ever win again, but just stay the course and keep hustlin'. Trust in the data, NO MATTER WHAT IT SAYS, rather than trusting in your own gut feelings. As crazy as it sounds, I'd rather lose with the data and going against myself than the other way around. The mental toll for losing on your own and not following the data isn't for me. Remember, this is a **Side Hustle**, not life and death. But the money is serious, and so is losing.

Fact: If you can't handle losing at sports gambling financially AND mentally, this won't end well for you.

We are all competitive on some levels. Some of us are more competitive than others, but if you are betting on sports then you like to win. Wagering on sports is not for slaps and tickles! This is serious business. You may be smiling and having fun, but the books are waiting on you to lose. Being able to cope with losing is far more important that celebrating the wins.

It's depressing to me that I'm a little too old for a few things these days. I remember when we only had 4 TV channels, and they were connected to rabbit ears. If the president was speaking, every channel showed it and we were screwed. I remember a time when we didn't even have the internet in every home. But maybe the most depressing aspect of being born at the wrong time is being too old for the E-Sports Revolution. If they have out college scholarships in my day for sports video games, I could have graduated at the top of any Ivy League school.

Nintendo RBI Baseball is probably my favorite all-time video game. Most people of my age group will go with Tecmo Bowl, and NBA Jam had its moment. But RBI Baseball was the first video game that used the real names of real players and gave them their characteristics. For example, Andre Dawson was the best player on the game. And in 1987, Dawson was the MVP of the National League while playing on a last place Chicago Cubs team. Sure, every player looked exactly the same. Tall players looked the same as shorter players. White players had the same skin tone as black players. Players with long last names had them abbreviated to where you had to know them to identify them. Someone named Al Pedrique and his 449 career at bats was deemed a National League All-Star. But nobody cared! We finally had a game with real players and their real names and abilities for the first time, instead of guys with generic names.

And in those days, hanging out with a bunch of guys usually ended in calling it a night earlier than planned and going back to challenge each other at sports video games. And the game of choice was what was in season: baseball in the summer, football in the fall and winter, and basketball in the spring. Good times! Both in Kentucky and in Atlanta, I'd go out with friends and we'd get so fired up about beating each other at that game that we would leave parties early and bars before closing time to get in some action. Yes, we were nerds, or losers, or whatever you want to call us. At least we stayed out of trouble. Oh well, bragging rights and "buckets of pride" were usually the only things on the line.

But on occasion, there would be some cash or something of value up for grabs. Those were when the feelings got hurt. In fact, that was when the phrase "pulling a Brad" was invented. In Tecmo Bowl, there were only a few plays to choose from on a play-by-play basis. If the defense guessed the exact play the offense called, it would be a "jailbreak" play of chaos that always ended badly for the offense. Sometimes, I might have shifted my eyes to peek at the hands of my opponent to see which offensive play they were calling, then calling the same play myself to get an advantage. However, I never did this nearly as often as I was accused! This led to everyone who played to play with a towel or pillow over their hands in their laps to hide the play calling from anyone who might have eyes that stray in the slightest. It's always a good thing when a rule is named after you, except in this example.

SIDE HUSTLE

In an early 90's summer, when I was back in Kentucky for summer break from school, I was out one night. Lo and behold, I see some guys I hadn't seen in years. Lots of smiles and lots of laughs were shared in a long period of time that seemed like just a few minutes. Then as closing time approached, those guys I hadn't seen for a while said they were getting back to their shared place to play RBI Baseball. What a shock! More guys my age that played the same video games that I did. I extended a challenge, and you would have thought I'd insulted their mothers! Those were fightin' words! How dare you claim you can beat any of us at RBI Baseball! They asked me how much money I wanted to bet on a series of RBI, and I said "how about $20?" Keep in mind, at that time in my life, $20 might as well have been $20,000. I needed the cash! So we all drove back to their place for an "Envelope Game." An Envelope Game was a wager placed where the money had to be submitted before the event took place, whether it was a Friday night video game, or the Super Bowl. This was done because you simply didn't trust your opponent to pay up if they lose. And among my friends in Kentucky, I didn't trust a single one of them when it came to matters like this!

So, my friend that I hadn't seen in years welcomed me to his home to play RBI Baseball. Good times, right? Not at all. There was a lot of good-natured professional wrestling-type trash talk as we started, but that was about to change. I realized that I was going to beat him rather early in the best 2 out of 3 series of games. My friend's trash talking had gone from funny to mean. And his friends, who were openly rooting for him and against me, were even more upset than he was. After winning the first game, I easily had the strategic advantage due to him burning all his starting pitchers in Game 1. The atmostphere had become somewhat toxic to the point that by the time the 2nd game began, I was planning my quick escape after winning.

But my friend was truly furious. I had never seen anyone that angry over losing a video game. Sure, I got pissed off at times when I lost, but never to this extent. Suddenly, my friend turned to physical violence of furniture. And his friends, who had seen this act from him before, cleared out because they knew it was over and didn't want to be around to see his act. In this game, when a team gets a lead of 10 runs or more, the game automatically ended in a "skunk" rule ending. As my guy hit a home run to end the series, I wanted to get out of there immediately. But as the ball was flying out of the park, my friend ripped the Nintendo controller off the wire and threw it as hard as he could. The controller was destroyed. Those controllers were about $20 at the time. As the game ended, I grabbed my $20 out of the envelope, told him to use the other $20 to get another controller, and got out of there as quickly as I could. I jogged to my car and drove away. But looking at his house as I left, I could see him on his front porch as he was yelling obscenities at me. As much as I needed the $20 at the time, I didn't have the heart to take the kid's money.

As fate would have it, I never saw that kid again. But when a mutual friend of ours passed away at a young age a year or so later, he saw a friend of mine and sent word through him that he was truly sorry about that night. But the lesson here has stuck with me for over 3 decades now: how we handle losing is very important. It's not just important to us, but it's important the ones who care about us. Whether it's your better half, your family, or even your pets. We need to be able to be the same whether we are on a big winning streak or a big losing streak. If people close to you can tell when you're winning or losing, you're doing this wrong.

Some of the best sports gamblers in the world will tell you that the best friend someone can have during a losing streak is a dog. Dogs are always loyal, and they don't care if you win or lose. They're thrilled to see you every time you come home. Their happiness doesn't have anything to do with your bankroll. That's always reassuring and can always take the stress of losing away a little. It also helps bring us back to reality because there are times when we as sports gamblers can get in a little too deep. On a college basketball Saturday in January and February, it can be easy to get too caught up in lines and results. But there's your dog, loyal and faithful as ever, to make you smile even if you lost on a 90-feet Hail Mary shot in overtime. It seems silly, but pets can help deal with losing, because mine have always helped get over the sting.

The RBI Story is also a reminder that when we think we are the best at something, somebody comes along and puts us in our place. This especially goes for sports gambling. None of us Squares will ever be the best, but we are just trying to make a profit as a **Side Hustle**.

What happens when we lose? We have those crazy self-talk thoughts:

I'm the biggest loser, ever.

My family is ashamed of me.

I'll never win again.

It's easy to get caught up in negative thoughts in times like this. And if you turn to booze or drugs, it might get worse! If we can get through the losing streak, the winning streak is on the way. The trick is staying even keeled until that happens because it will.

BOTTOM LINE

Losing is inevitable, but it happens to all of us. As sports gamblers, we can be defined by how we react to losing. Do we quit? Do we dismiss it as rigged? Do we take it out on others? One bet should NEVER change your life. If it does, you aren't doing this the right way, even if you hit that impossible 10-team parlay that the sports books "leak" to the media.

SIDE HUSTLE

13
THE *JEOPARDY!* DILEMMA

Exhibit A that some of the smartest people in the world can be some of the dumbest gamblers.

"All-in, Alex!" - James Holzhauer, many times on "Jeopardy!"

Don't lie! You watch *Jeopardy!* from time to time. We all do. In fact, one of the greatest moments in game show history was when there was a category on the NFL and none of the 3 contestants correctly answered any of the 5 questions in the entire category. Even the late Alex Trebek was cracking jokes at their football knowledge shortcomings!

But watching this show reminds me that there truly is a difference between "Book Smart" and "Street Smart." My dad always made fun of me when I was a kid, saying that I was only book smart and could never make it in the real world. I was a kid! And I grew up on a farm in Kentucky! Where the heck am I going to get these "Street Smarts" you speak of, sir? The only street smarts I had were "Sesame Street Smarts." Oh, don't worry. I got it in Atlanta for 20-something years, but that's another story for another day.

But *Jeopardy!* isn't a show that makes you feel better about yourself very often, unless you can answer all the questions. One of my most satisfying moments watching game shows ever was when

SIDE HUSTLE

Ken Jennings was on his original run of 74 wins in a row, but I got the final question that he missed to lose and go home. I felt smart for at least one day, anyway. But this game show can also make a sports gambler feel better about themselves.

James Holzhauer was on the show in 2019 for 33 episodes. It doesn't seem like that long ago, and it seems like he was on longer than that. But *Jeopardy!* James, as he was called, truly changed the game. Most people would pick a category and go straight down from top to bottom. But James knew the randomly hidden Daily Doubles gave the contestant who found it much power. The contestant who finds the Daily Double can wager on that question, instead of the game telling you how much it's worth. James would intentionally skip the easy, low value questions and immediately start looking for the Daily Doubles. Quite often, he found them. And quite often, he took advantage of them. Most of his games were decided before the first commercial break, only 15 questions into the game which had 61 questions total. James broke records for amounts won in one episode several times. It was exciting to watch someone that dominant.

But what made James so dominant was that also knew how to bet. Why? He was a sports gambler. So many times, I have watched *Jeopardy!* and absolutely yelled obscenities at the television when people make dumb wagers. I can promise you that I've gotten more upset at *Jeopardy!* wagers than any sporting event on which I've wagered. And it's not even close! The Final *Jeopardy!* bets are the worst! How many times has someone in 2nd or 3rd place going into the final question just need to bet nothing and they will win if the others get it wrong? Yet, every night, someone screws up. When it happens, I can hear my dad's voice telling me how "Book Smart" people don't have "Street Smarts." Like most of the ridiculous assumptions he made about me, that couldn't be more wrong. *Jeopardy!* James is proof.

He changed the game. And although there were some before him that tried (Arthur Chu being one of the O.G.'s of this strategy), James was the best. And now, he's parlayed that into even bigger things. Not bad for a Book Smart nerd who knew how to gamble on sports, huh?

As the years have passed since James was on *Jeopardy!*, there have been many copycats. Maybe it was that James was the first contestant to have the nerve to play it differently. Whatever it was, there are plenty of copycats on the show today. If I see someone begin a round by choosing the minimum value question on the top row, I immediately cross that contestant off the list of potential winners.

But there's a positive lesson to be learned in watching these horrible gamblers on *Jeopardy!* They can't gamble to save their lives. In fact, some of them can't gamble to save their *Jeopardy!* careers. If some of the smartest "Book Smart" people in the world have no idea how to bet on that show, that means a lot of smart people in this world can be terrible sports gamblers. We don't have to be geniuses to bet on sports, but we need to be Sharp. Again, sports gambling is hard or else these "Book Smart" people would do it too. Take solace in the fact that intelligent people often look like Squares when betting Daily Doubles!

The fact that *Jeopardy!* contestants can be such bad gamblers tells us something: this is an acquired talent. We can't just go into this expecting to be the very best from the beginning. We can read all the books in the world, but experience is the best teacher. You'll learn more from gambling for a year than you ever will in a book. Even *Jeopardy!* James will tell you that.

SIDE HUSTLE

BOTTOM LINE

You're not alone in being a bad gambler. Even some of the smartest and most intelligent people in the world are the worst gamblers. Don't feel bad that you don't know everything about gambling. Try to get better every day at it. Just by reading this book, you're at least on your way. All you need to do is watch *Jeopardy!* and you'll see some of the worst gamblers ever! And just like back in the day when watching those daytime talk shows, it will make you feel a little better about how good you've got it (especially during a losing streak). The lie detector test has determined that you can win at sports gambling!

14
SQUARE THINKING vs. SHARP THINKING:

The Eternal Struggle.

"There are two kinds of people in the world: people who laugh at fart jokes, and people who do not." - Brad Taylor.

I believe this wholeheartedly. What does it say for my family that my dad thought fart jokes were awful, and my mom laughed hysterically at them. I have no idea, but it was an eternal struggle for them as well.

In fact, I knew a guy in college named Lance. One day he came into school just fuming with some Aqua Velva knock-off that you can get a gallon for 50 cents, and they'll give you a free bowl of soup with it, too! We all said hello to Lance, while wondering what that aroma was. As he walked away, I whispered to my friends around me at the time, "Lance? More like Flatu-Lance!" Lance had his nickname, and it stuck with him until we got out of school. Years later, Lance saw one of my old friends and he asked how I was doing. Needless to say, he still is not happy with me giving him his college nickname. But he didn't have to drown himself in that stuff, sheesh! When I saw *Anchorman* with the Sex Panther cologne, I immediately flashed back to Flatu-Lance! It was the exact same thing!

Anyway, along with the fart jokes, there are also 2 kinds of people in this sports gambling world: Sharps and Squares. We want to think like Squares, but we must think like Sharps to win long term. Sports gambling is one of the most difficult things to change the way we have been conditioned to think over the years. But if you think about it, if you're losing long term, you really do need to change the way you think!

Over the years, I have known a few Sharps, but I have known a LOT of Squares. The Sharps are not smarter than the Squares, per se. They just think differently. I know this because there was a time when I was a big Square as well. But when you get figuratively punched in the face enough times, eventually you put your hands up to protect yourself. In other words, you lose enough as a Square that you either become a Sharp or get out of the game altogether. As Squares, we have to change everything we've been conditioned to believe and start thinking like Sharps.

Below are some differences I've noticed over the years between the Pros and Joes of sports gambling:

SQUARES love to play the favorites and go over totals.
SHARPS love to play the underdogs and go under totals.

The best teams in any sports are always overrated and overvalued in the desert. Throughout this book, you will see that underdogs have a better winning percentage against the spread than favorites do. That doesn't mean that blindly playing all favorites is the way to go, but we can find spots where the underdogs are the play much more than favorites.

In addition, the public is always on the favorites. Look at betting splits, and invariably we will find that most of the Squares are on the favored team. And the bigger the game, the more the Squares run to play the favorite that everyone else is playing.

Favorites lose for 3 main reasons: Underdog Psychology, too much money comes in on the best teams, and the public loves the best teams.

Underdog Psychology comes all the way from David. The public embraces the favorites and gives the underdogs no chance. If someone tells you that you aren't as good as someone else, doesn't it fire you up to compete and do better? It should. And it certainly does in the sports world. How many times have we heard coaches or players tell the media after an upset "None of you gave us a chance to win! We showed you!" And what does the favorite think? They think that if the media thinks we can't lose, then we can't lose. I love taking the biggest of underdogs: teams on losing streaks, teams the public think have no chance, huge underdogs against the point spread. Those are my ticket cashers. Even The Statue of Liberty says "Give me your tired, your poor, Your huddled masses yearning to breathe free, The wretched refuse of your teeming shore." That goes for us sports gamblers too. Give me the teams that everyone else doesn't want. Those are the teams that get me over 52.38%.

The best teams are ALWAYS overrated. There are 32 teams in the NFL. The difference between team #1 and team #16 is miniscule. And the difference between team #1 and team #32 is probably one player (usually a quarterback), or one coach. If the defending Super Bowl champ with an established quarterback and legendary coach face a team with a rookie quarterback and rookie head coach, who is going to bet on the underdog here? The public will race each other to the window to get their action down on the favorite. But betting on the best teams is a bad choice. The point spread evens the playing field where the massive underdgos are better plays. The public just doesn't realize it.

The public loves betting favorites. Check out betting splits. It speaks for themselves. The public loves to bet "overs" when it comes to totals as well. Check out the betting splits on those! The public doesn't root against teams to score! They're having a good time! Enjoying life! We love the high scoring, flashy offenses. Unders cash more than Overs: **Bottom Line**!

SQUARES will play the BIG underdogs and parlays in the hopes of hitting one big ticket.

SHARPS grind out profits with straight –110 (or less) bets on a daily basis, and every single day.

Every week or so during football season, we will hear about Person A hitting a crazy 15-team parlay on an NFL weekend. The sports books are the ones who release that information to the media, not the bettor. You've heard of Mattress Mack? He's owns the Gallery Furniture retail chain. He is based in Houston, and often offers promos based on the local teams in the Houston area. To ""ensure"" his promos so he doesn't get taken to the proverbial cleaners, he will place large 7-figure bets to hedge his investments. But Mattress Mack isn't the one who publicize these bets. The sports books are.

Hope is a great quality that anyone can have. If you think about it, why are we even trying every day if we don't have hope! We have to have at least some. But in sports gambling, hope can be the worst thing that bad sports gamblers possess if you don't know how to use it.

A sports gambler came up to me once and asked why I bet only straight bets. How about future odds where you can get a team to win a championship at huge odds with a huge payoff? And you might hit a big future, but you'll lose a bunch of future bets trying to find that winner. That's why in PGA Golf wagering, I will only bet matchups between Player A and Player B, and not Player C to win the tournament at 20/1. I'm trying to grind out a profit here. If I wanted quick action with big winners and losers, I'd head to the craps table.

And even when making straight bets, watch the juice. A lot of the Square books will offer a half point better odds than the other books, but kill you with the vig. Would you rather have Team A at +4, -110? Or would you rather have Team A at +4.5, -120? The value is with Team A at +4, -110. I'm not laying any juice for any straight bet on a side or total of more than −110. If you have no choice, then have the discipline to pass.

SQUARES don't have a solid game plan and get games as they come.

SHARPS are extremely calculated and plan everything.

I went to Las Vegas many years ago for the first weekend of the NCAA Tournament. One of my friends who joined me promised his wife that he wouldn't tap the ATM card if he went broke. Not exactly the best situation, but we can work around it. We spent the entire flight from Atlanta to Las Vegas going over how to do this, especially money management and betting amounts per wager.

As the Tournament started, this guy was going to follow me on all my basketball picks. It's a 4-day marathon, with Thursday and Friday being 16-game days with plenty of action. As we started on Thursday, we won our first 3 games. Good times! Then we lost the next 2. OK, so we are 3-2, winning 60%. Still a winner and a profit for the day. With the next wave of games starting, my friend says he is going back to the room. I said no way! We are just getting started and we have more than 3 ½ days to go! Then he quietly told me he was out of money. He won his first 3 bets, and thought we were never going to lose again. After betting a little in the first 3 games, he went all in on the last 2. So, while I'm sitting there with more money than I started with, he was broke. I had a plan. He didn't.

To win at this, you have to grind out winners against the sports book. Bet the same amount on every game, look for mostly underdogs/under totals, and only bet games where you have data-based information proven to be profitable over long periods of time. Never go "All In" or "Double or Nothing" on any sports wager, regardless of the circumstance. The sports gambling world is filled with guys who can hit 55% winners for a period of time, yet somehow are able to still lose money in the process. The biggest reason for that is having no plan or money management.

SQUARES are satisfied with one betting account because a half point here and there doesn't matter.

SHARPS have many betting accounts because a half point here and there can mean a lot.

The books want your business. If you win big at the tables in Las Vegas, they give you plenty of goodies and luxuries because they want to keep you there to get their money back at the tables eventually. If you are shopping for a car, and you can get the same car $1,000 cheaper at one dealership than another. You're probably going to buy from the place that offers it $1,000 cheaper, right?

The same goes for sports books. They all want your business. But most Squares will only open up one account and go from there. That's a mistake! Get down with every sports book you can, taking care of their sign-up bonuses in the process, so you can have several outs and options for any wager you make. If you think a half point doesn't make a difference, you're wrong. It might not matter tonight, but it will long term. And not taking advantage of what little the books give you is a mistake. Sign up for as many accounts as you can and compare the odds before making a wager. Your bankroll will thank you.

SQUARES like to follow the crowd believing in "Strength In Numbers."

SHARPS love being in the minority and against the Squares.

This is called "gambling." It's not "sure-fire money." The Square looks to follow others. They want to bet the same thing their friends bet, so that if they lose then everyone loses. As the saying goes, "misery loves company."

The public uses a lot of "eye tests" and "gut instincts." Those are two of my favorite reasons to NOT bet on a team. If all your friends, family, and even the guys you share a pop with at the bar are on one team, that's a sure sign to go the other way. Does that mean they are stupid? No. It means they are just like the rest of the public: Squares who don't win in the desert long term. They know nothing, and neither do you or I. And most "experts" just parrot (or imitate) things they hear from the media.

SQUARES believe as long as they can pick winners, everything else will work itself out. Just don't go on a losing streak!

SHARPS can still "tread water" during losing streaks, unlike the Squares.

What do Sharps and Squares have in common? They both go on gigantic losing streaks at times. The Squares fall apart and vanish from the sports betting world. The Sharps not only survive, but they flourish. When on a losing streak, keep swinging the bat just as hard the next day. The Sharps realize that. The Squares live in fear, and it gets the best of them. Here's another spot where Money Management is so important. Bet a minimal percentage of your bankroll on every bet and make it the same amount every bet.

SQUARES have unrealistic expectations. And when they can't pull off a miracle, it's over.

SHARPS know how difficult this is. And when they go on a losing streak, they continue grinding.

I once told a co-worker that I had won 53% of my bets during college basketball season. To me, that's great! To him, he laughed hysterically and called me a "loser." Excuse me? Are you doing better than 53% in a 5-month college basketball season? If so, I'd like to see how you do it! But the co-worked just assumed that hitting 53% was awful and told me that if I wasn't hitting 60% that I shouldn't even waste my time. Fair enough! Strike another Square off my list of people to discuss sports gambling with on a daily basis.

It's like the casino: any day you walk out of a casino with a penny more than you walked in with was a good day. The same goes for sports gambling.

SQUARES bet on their favorite teams to have a rooting interest.

SHARPS look at each game as Team A vs. Team B.

Unbiased handicapping: once a sports gambler can truly master this, that's when the winning can begin. I deal with a lot of fans of local teams. Those fans are destined to be sports betting losers because they will only bet for, and never against, their favorite teams. My mentality is that I can bet on Team A one night and bet against that same Team A the next night, and not blink an eye.

SIDE HUSTLE

SQUARES are often impatient and go for broke after a certain period of time (whether winning or losing).

SHARPS know "Patience is a Virtue," and never throw the Hail Mary.

"It's the first quarter of the big game and you wanna toss up a hail mary?" - Vince Vaughn in Wedding Crashers

This is a slow play, for the long term. If you want to bet the Super Bowl and get out, that's fair enough. But most of us bet on games throughout each season. Betting more than 5% of your bankroll at one time is a quick way to end your sports betting career earlier than you thought. Patience, young grasshopper! I never bet more than 1% of my bankroll per wager. It's called having "staying power."

SQUARES look at lines and make their bets. No need to do a lot of research if they know who they're betting.

SHARPS do all kinds of research and can make data-based handicapping decisions.

For those who just look at the lines, ask who the home team is, the make their bets, they don't last long either. On a January or February Saturday, I'm looking at well over 100 college basketball games, all of which can be potentially profitable. A good sports gambler will run their numbers and systems on every game to find an advantage, not just look at a line with conventional wisdom and hope.

SQUARES listen to the media because they are "insiders." They have more knowledge than anyone.

SHARPS don't listen to the media, gather their own information, and handicap games based on numbers and data, not cliche' and hearsay.

Super Bowl 25 was between the New York Giants and the Buffalo Bills. Yes, the Scott Norwood game. The week before the Super Bowl, all the media could say was that the Bills were the greatest team ever since they had won the AFC Championship by a score of 51-3, while the Giants had won on a field goal on the last play of the game. By the way, people sleep on the 1990 NFC Championship Game between the Giants and the San Francisco 49ers on being as good as any game ever, but I digress.

But I fell for the hype! I gave up on the Giants and played the Bills. It was only because the media had convinced me to do so. Lesson learned. Never again! The next year, the 1991 UNLV basketball team taught us a very similar lesson. I didn't fall for the banana in the tail pipe trick that time!

SQUARES make bets whenever they get the time, regardless of the point spread at that moment.

SHARPS will bet games as they are released to the public, or strategically wait online moves to benefit them.

A good rule of thumb: if you're going to bet a favorite, bet them as early as you can. If you're going to bet an underdog, wait as long as you can before the game starts to place your wager. This won't work every time, but it will work more than half of the time. The logic is that the public bets favorites. The longer the public has to get their money down on the favorites, the more potential value the underdog may have. This especially works in football when lines will come out several days before the games.

Timing is everything! Look for betting trends and betting splits to help you know the best time to place a bet. Like most things in life, it's better to be a little early than a little late.

SQUARES don't care what happened yesterday because they only care about what happens today.

SHARPS realize those who don't learn from the past are doomed to repeat it.

Living through the windshield, not the rear-view mirror! I use a lot of historical and statistical data when handicapping games. What else is a Sharp going to use? The Eye Test? The cut of their jib? Using systems that cover many years and hundreds of games in a sample size can improve your **Bottom Line** very quickly.

SQUARES like those shiny new offensive teams that everyone fawns over.

SHARPS love a good ugly defense that doesn't get the hype.

"Defense wins championships!" We have heard that all our lives when it comes to sports. And while the sports world sees the offensive powerhouses more favorably these days, the desert still loves the defenses. In fact, defenses still offer much more value than the high-octane offenses. In the first round of the NCAA Tournament, those small teams with good defenses are like gold, and are often way underpriced in the desert. The Squares look for offense, but the Sharps look for defense.

SQUARES love to bet football. Well, because it's football and everybody bets football.

SHARPS will bet any sport that makes them money.

We all know the NFL is king, but that doesn't mean you have to bet it. The NFL is a tough sport to master. I have more success in college football and college basketball. And I don't even bet NBA regular season games anymore. As sports gamblers, we don't have to bet every major sport in season. Bet the sports you have the most success with and go full speed. Choosing 1 or 2 sports to bet on can improve your **Bottom Line** with quality over quantity. Take 1 or 2 sports and make them yours!

SQUARES feel as if they have to watch every game to be an expert.
SHARPS don't even have to watch the games to profit.
How does a true Sharp make money in this world? Make money while you sleep. We don't have to watch every single game we bet. In fact, I rarely do it these days. The data and the box scores give me the information better than my eyes can. And our eyes are biased! They lie to us all the time, especially when it comes to sports. Just because you can't name the #4 and #5 guys in the starting rotations in the AL West, that doesn't mean you will never win at sports gambling.

SQUARES do not need to keep track of my bets. "I just look at my account balance to see how I'm doing."
SHARPS not only do I keep track of their bets but learn from their many mistakes.
I run an Excel spreadsheet on a daily basis keeping track of the bets I make and don't make, along with the best I win and lose. I know the sports I bet better than the others and play them more. I also know which sports in which I struggle and will act accordingly.
Sharps will study their sports gambling history and act accordingly, playing to their strengths. Squares will ignore their history and keep making the same mistakes repeatedly.

SQUARES believe what their eyes tell them. Their "Eye Test" beats all the data.

SHARPS believe in the data more than their own eyes.

If reading the chapter on the 1989 NCAA Tournament didn't convince you where I stand on this, nothing will. I'm a Square. You're a Square. But the data can help transform us into Sharps if you trust the numbers more than you trust yourself.

SQUARES When betting point or run totals, always look to go over because it's no fun rooting against teams to score.

SHARPS Look to take unders because they cash more tickets than overs long term. It's fine to root against human achievement.

There are t-shirts floating around gambling circles with the saying "Life's too short to bet on the under." Possibly true, in theory, but life can last longer with the money you make betting on the under. Nobody usually likes to root against human achievement, but the Sharps do. As you will see later in this book, unders cash more than overs. Do with that what you will.

SQUARES love betting the home teams instead of visiting teams.

SHARPS always look to take road teams over home teams, if possible.

History tells us that road teams cover more point spreads and cash more tickets in all the major sports. This is due to the public overvaluing home advantages. When a Square wants to know about a game, the first question they will ask is, "Who is the home team?" Then, they will side with them. Squares will also tell you "Home teams get an automatic 3 points in the desert." Does LSU or Clemson football have the same 3-point home field advantage as Vanderbilt? Not even close....

SIDE HUSTLE

SQUARES don't need to start with a big bankroll. If they start hot, they can build up a huge profit from a very small beginning.

SHARPS build an initial bankroll as high as possible, playing as if they are going to lose every penny so it will not change their lives.

Saving money for an initial bankroll might take a minute. Sure, you can start with a few hundred dollars. But if you do, you probably should be wagering less than $10 per game. Squares think they need to wager more than that because they need the sweat. Sharps don't need the sweat. They just want the money. If you want to bet big, your bankroll needs to be big as well. Otherwise, this might end ugly and quickly for you.

SQUARES just saw Team A on television last week and they looked great! Team B looked lousy! How come Team B is favored this week?

SHARPS Recency bias is a helluva drug

The desert does not make mistakes with lines. And just because a team looked great last week, it doesn't mean they will continue that this week. The NFL is notorious for teams looking like world beaters one day, and a high school team the next. It's part of why the NFL might be the most difficult sport to handicap. It's better to handicap a lot more than just last week's results.

BOTTOM LINE

If there's a chapter in this book that will change your way of thinking, this is it. Don't be a Square! Be a Sharp! We are conditioned to think like a Square, sadly. So, it takes a little hustle to overcome how we were raised. And don't forget these wonderful words of wisdom: he who smelt it, dealt it.

15
DONT BE A PELPHREY

Scared money doesn't make money!

Disclaimer: I have never met the character in question for this chapter, John Pelphrey. Also, I have nothing against he, or anyone else associated with University of Kentucky Basketball. I'm simply using an event that took place several decades ago as an analogy for sports gambling. The Big Blue Nation (aka University of Kentucky fans) from back in his day love the guy from his basketball playing days at Kentucky, and rightly so. He's one of the most beloved players in the history of the program, and deservedly so. His jersey is hanging from the rafters at storied Rupp Arena. But one moment in time can sometimes determine what you think about someone. I'm sure I will hear a lot of feedback on this from the Kentucky fans, but it's only done to prove a point for this book.

Growing up in Central Kentucky, and then moving back in my 40's, it's all about Kentucky Basketball. Sure, there are other local sports here, Kentucky Football, the Reds, and the Bengals have their devoted fans, but people in Lexington could talk college hoops 365 days a year. Thankfully, I can talk college basketball only about 5 months a year. That's all I can take before going crazy!

In 1992, possibly the greatest shot in the history of college basketball took place in the NCAA Tournament. Duke's Christian

SIDE HUSTLE

Laettner hit a shot as the buzzer sounded to defeat Kentucky in the Elite 8 round. Duke was the defending national champion and #1 seed, while Kentucky was making their first Tournament appearance since 1988. The state of Kentucky loved that team more than any other in my lifetime, including national championship teams. Books have been written, documentaries have been made, and many have cashed in on this event, arguably the greatest college basketball game ever played. By the way, Kentucky covered the spread as a 7.5-point underdog in this one, but I digress.

Every March, CBS goes through the cob webs in their basement and trots out that VHS tape (non-HD) of Laettner's shot to remind people of the drama of the Tournament. But what nobody ever talks about in this whole thing is John Pelphrey. Laettner had a perfect night going up to that point, 9 for 9 shots from field, 10 of 10 from the free throw line. Allegedly, Kentucky Coach Rick Pitino had ordered Pelphrey and Deron Feldhaus to double team Laettner. Feldhaus held up his end, but Pelphrey didn't. As Laettner catches the in-bounds pass, Pelphrey is right there to challenge the pass. In fact, Pelphrey bumps Laettner in the air as the ball is caught by Laettner. Instead of challenging Laettner, Pelphrey becomes timid. And there is the mistake: As Laettner catches the ball and gathers himself to put up his shot, Pelphrey backs away. In fact, Pelphrey drops his arms, backs up, and appears to be looking at the clock/scoreboard high above center court as Laettner is fighting to get his shot off right next to him. You can see him, #34 in blue, in the picture above. Pelphrey is just watching as Laettner shoots what should be a very contested shot but isn't. Once the shot goes in, Pelphrey's shoulders drop. And for that matter, so does everyone's in the state of Kentucky.

That game took place on a Saturday night. For days, the lead story on the local television news after that game in Lexington had nothing to do with news. It had to do with reaction to that game. Why didn't Kentucky coach Rick Pitino guard Grant Hill taking the ball out of bounds? Why wasn't Laettner at least given a technical foul, if not ejected, when he literally stomped on a Kentucky player? What are these senior players going to do now? Legendary radio announcer Cawood Ledford was retiring and announced his final Kentucky basketball game that night as it turned out, but he was broadcasting the Final Four the following weekend for national radio. Before the National Championship Game, Ledford was asked what it was going to be like broadcasting his final game. He said "I've already broadcasted my last game." Kentucky basketball is a big deal, and that game was a big deal. And it still is to many people in the Bluegrass State.

It's one of those moments where most Kentuckians know exactly where they were when it happened. I remember where I was. I was out in Atlanta watching the game with friends. In fact, most of them had ties to Kentucky and they were celebrating the potential win. There were also Duke fans where we were, and they were jawing with us until Kentucky was leading with 2 seconds left. At that time, one of my friends went to the bar where the bartender was a fellow student of ours. How do you think we were able to afford a night out? You gotta know somebody who can help you out! Anyway, my friend tells the bartender to open a bottle of victory champagne and have it ready when those last 2 seconds end so we can have a toast to the victors, and stick it to those Duke fans. The bartender, who was also sick of hearing the Duke people all night, smiled and said he'd be happy to let us have the last bottle of champagne in the house when the game was over. It seemed a little much for a college basketball game, but I wasn't going to say "no" to free champagne! Of course, we know what happened next. Our friend the bartender came over to our table after the shot, where everyone was still in shock, and asked us "The Duke fans asked for the bottle of champagne. Can I let them buy it?" My friend slides the bartender a $50 bill and said, "Poor it down the f---ing drain right in front of them and tell them we did it." Talk about ballsy! We immediately packed up and left while the bartender poured the champagne out. The Duke fans weren't happy about that, and yelled at us as we were leaving, leading to several gestures telling them they're Number 1 with a certain finger, if you know what I mean. As we got in cars to leave, not much was said for several minutes until someone said, "Did you really tell the bartender to pour it down the f---ing drain?" That led to all of us laughing. And just like that, we were over it. Life goes on.

But we were in the minority. We got over it that night. There are people in Kentucky to this day who STILL aren't over that game, played so long ago now. The hatred was so much, that when Duke played Indiana in an NCAA Tournament game in Lexington in 2002, the entire 23,000+ in attendance was rooting for Indiana. Wait a minute! Kentucky and Indiana were bitter basketball rivals in the 70's and 80's. If you had told any Kentucky fan at any time before 1992 that Lexington would be unanimously for Indiana over Duke in basketball, they would have called you crazy.

Ok, Mr. **Side Hustle** Guy. That's a great story, but what does all this Laettner shot junk have to do with winning sports bets? As I've gotten older, I sometimes go back to this moment and think to myself "don't be a Pelphrey." Take risks in life! Luck is a myth. It's when opportunity meets preparation.

It's also a lesson in holding on to the past. In sports gambling, we MUST not let the previous day's betting results determine how we bet today. If I go on a losing streak, that means my hot streak is just around the corner. So, let's get up off the floor, and swing for the fences today just like when we struck out yesterday. A great attitude is to look at a losing streak as a GOOD thing, because that means the hot streak comeback is coming sooner and more profitable than we thought. We just have to stick to our guns and keep grinding, because it WILL happen.

Betting in fear will never work. Making decisions on your own will hold you back as well. If the data says one thing, and you chicken out because you are thinking another thing, that's a sure-fire way to lose long term. This is called gambling. It's not safe investing. There is a risk in every wager we make. That's why I make sure that one bet never changes my life, for bettor or worse. If you ever get to a point where you are scared of making bets, this isn't the **Side Hustle** for you.

If we approach this 75% of what we have, we will never make it. It takes 100% dedication to the grind to win at this long term. Can you lose 5 nights in a row and wake up the 6th day ready to pick 100% winners that day? And can you have the same enthusiasm when you're losing? It's easy to get up in the morning when you're on a winning streak and check your numbers. It's a lot harder when you're on a losing streak. Can you get up with the same enthusiasm every day? That's what it takes to win at sports gambling.

Sports gamblers are risk takers because we have to be. Risk takers in life take chances and don't settle for an ordinary life. Making sports gambling your **Side Hustle** is Step 1 in taking risk in your life. Now, we just have to start cashing tickets and turning a profit, which is easier said than done.

SIDE HUSTLE

BOTTOM LINE

Watching John Pelphrey react to that Christian Laettner shot is something that I've remembered for over 3 decades now. I'm not upset about the result, but I remember that someone would watch the clock hoping it would run out instead of doing something yourself about it. Sports gambling isn't for the timid. Hoping you'll win isn't Sharp thinking. And if you are truly going to do this long term, you can't "half-ass" it. You have to go "all in." If you can't handle the ups and downs involved in this, then it's a good idea to find another **Side Hustle**. When I say, "all in," that's every day, no matter what, 361 days a year (I take 4 days in July off every year). If you don't, and only do it when you feel like it or when circumstances allow it, there are other **Side Hustle**s out there that are a better fit.

16
THE PRIVATE VICTORIES IN LIFE

The best wins are often the ones that nobody else can celebrate with us.

"Act like you've been there before." - Vince Lombardi.

Barry Sanders was one of the greatest running backs of all time. The sports talk radio argument in the early/mid 90's was, "who was the better running back? Emmitt Smith or Barry Sanders?" Bo Jackson was better in Tecmo Bowl, but that only mattered on Friday nights after school. It truly helped Smith that he played on one of the greatest teams of all-time, with one of the greatest offensive lines of all-time. What is Sanders played for those Dallas teams? And Emmitt played for those Detroit teams? Sanders was better.

But what Sanders had over Smith was touchdown celebrations. Emmitt Smith kept every touchdown ball he ever scored in the NFL, took his helmet off before the league banned it, and celebrated every touchdown like it won a Super Bowl. Barry Sanders would just flip the ball to the referee and jog to the sidelines. Sanders acted like he had been there before. Sanders was better.

When the Chicago Cubs win a home game at Wrigley Field, they will fly the "W" Win Flag as seen above. It's a symbol to everyone that the Cubs actually won today. And for pedestrians walking outside of the stadium, they see the flag and smile that their team won the game.

SIDE HUSTLE

This started in 1937, when it actually was informative to people who didn't go to the game. Of course, in this day and age this seems prehistoric because we already know who wins these games less than 10 seconds after they end due to technology.

Sometimes, you will see people post their winning sports gambling tickets on social media. Floyd "Money" Mayweather was good at this for a while. Of course, this was the same guy who was given a check for $100 million after a fight and was carrying it in his coat pocket and showed it to the audience during a television interview. He requested the check instead of direct deposit, so that should tell you something. But have you ever noticed that these people never show losing tickets? Amzaing, huh? But he's not the only one! I've seen many people post their tickets AFTER the fact. How about posting them BEFORE the fact? THAT is the kind of shot caller we like: one who will tell you what he's betting before the wager is decided.

Effective individuals win two victories in life: a Private Victory when they learn self-mastery and self-discipline, and a Public Victory when they build deep and enduring relationships with others. "Life is about relationships," but not when it comes to sports gambling. This is where "Life is about cashing tickets," and nothing else.

But think about the greatest wins in your life. Were you surrounded by family and friends? Or were you alone? If you are a sports gambler, most of your wins are alone. They are the Private Victories, and they can make your bankroll bigger. As someone who bets on sports, I can speak from experience on this topic. We should NEVER let a bad bet, or a bad streak of bets, affect how we treat friends and family. That's where we can get in trouble. If we get on a losing streak, it's easy to blame anything that isn't you.

SIDE HUSTLE

On my radio show, I can promise you there are things the listeners don't want to hear about. They don't want to hear about my fantasy football team, and your brilliant free agent pickup in Week 9 that carried you to a championship. And they don't want to hear about a bet you won yesterday, or last week, or last year. Why is this? Because people don't want to hear stories of you succeeding in the past, they want help so they can win in the future. We don't live in the world anymore where we should recap what happened yesterday. Who cares? We already know! When a game ends, my phone lights up 3 seconds later with the results. Tell me what's going to happen tomorrow. That's the trick now.

Sports betting is not a popularity contest, although the Squares can treat it that way. If you go against your friends, you don't have to announce it. Ever go to a craps table at the casino? All the players are playing the "Pass Line" and rooting for the shooter. But every once in a while, there's that guy who bets on the "Don't Pass Line." In other words, the "Don't Pass Line" guy has no faith in the shooters at the table and is betting against everyone else. You're on an island, but that island isn't the dumbest place to be, game wise. It pisses off a lot of people, and it makes them unpopular, but that "Don't Pass Line" player has a slight advantage of winning more than the "Pass Line" player. Sure, he might he ridiculed when the shooter craps out, but he will also win when everyone else loses. Not many people have the guts to do such a thing in public. But unlike standing at the table and looking a shooter in the eye and proclaiming, "you stink, and I'm betting against you, loser!" We can bet on sporting events in private without enduring the insults of going against the public. Again, the private victories can be the ones we celebrate the most, especially in sports betting.

But I've learned that not only are people not very impressed with your sports betting wins, but they don't even want to hear about it. So, I don't share my wins with anyone. It's the Private Victories in life that can mean the most and be the most valuable for your bankroll.

The self-satisfaction of winning at sports gambling is something we can't beat. At the same time, it's not something we can go around bragging about to everyone because they will be turned off by it. It's a fine line between bragging, boasting, and just being darn good at what you do.

BOTTOM LINE

It's not a requirement that you have to go out and brag about your sports gambling winnings. Most people don't want to hear about your good fortune when they are still hustlin' themselves every day. In addition, the Gambling Gods tend to punish those who brag about their wins with a big losing streak. When you win at something as fickle as sports gambling, act like you've been there before because your fortunes can change in an instant.

17
FADING THE PUBLIC

Do the opposite of what you think, and what you see!

"If every instinct you have is wrong, then the opposite would have to be right." - Jerry Seinfeld to a downtrodden George Costanza on "Seinfeld".

Seinfeld doesn't age well visually. Jerry's wardrobe is unique, but somehow, he always got the hottest girls. It was amazing how that worked out like it did. But this goes down as one of my favorite sitcoms of all-time. A good friend from college who sadly is no longer with us, turned me on to this back in the very early 90's when nobody was watching it. From "The Contest" to The "Soup Nazi", to "The Merv Griffin Show", this is a show that I will still watch over a quarter century after it ended.

Another great episode was one called "The Opposite." George was frustrated with his life, and everything he did was wrong. Upon Jerry's sarcastic advice, George simply started doing the exact opposite of what he was doing before. One minute, George was an unemployed, bald man who lived with his parents. The next minute, George had a hot girlfriend, got a job with the New York Yankees, and moved out of his parents' house. Yes, this is a sitcom storyline. But there's a lot of validity to this line of thinking, especially in the world of sports gambling.

SIDE HUSTLE

How many people have tried to copy Michael Jordan over the years? From Kobe Bryant to LeBron James and many others, we've seen a lot of NBA players try to "Be Like Mike." That's fine, especially if you have as much talent as those guys. But remember that we can never be a complete copycat of a legend. In sports, especially coaching, we hear the adage, "You always want to replace the guy who replaced the legend, not replace the legend." In the NFL, Green Bay and San Francisco had the luck of having Hall of Fame quarterbacks replace Hall of Fame quarterbacks. The 49ers went from Joe Montana to Steve Young, and the Packers went from Brett Favre to Aaron Rodgers. But what made those "replacements" successful was that they were much different players and much different people than who they replaced. By the way, Steve Young gets no credit for being better than Joe Montana, but he was. Just look at the numbers. If I see Bill Walsh on the other side, that's the first question I'm asking him, because I know he agrees that Young was better than Montana, but I digress.

You can't completely copy what someone else has done. Not only that, do you want to fail doing it someone else's way? Or fail doing it your way? I'd choose the latter every time. But the real question is, "are you cut out to be a sports gambler and going against what everyone else is doing?" If you can't, you might want to find another **Side Hustle**.

I like to talk to people, public, squares, just guys who like sports and don't even like gambling. If money always on one side, go the other way. I like to listen to sports talk radio other than my show to get a feel. You can't win in life following the crowd. It just doesn't work. Too insecure and lack confidence to make their own choices and take their own path.

As sports gamblers, we should also look to be different than everyone else. I handicap games differently than most, and so should you. "Fading The Public" is a phrase often heard in sports gambling and has proven profitable over time. The bigger the game, the most the public gets their action down on that game. And the bigger the game, the more the public is usually wrong.

BOTTOM LINE

Contrarianism is a word, and it's a way of life in sports gambling. Not only that, but it works in the real world as well. If George Costanza can get a job with the New York Yankees (sort of), anything can happen. But going against conventional wisdom is a great way to get ahead in life, and especially sports gambling. Don't be afraid to fade the betting public at any time.

18
DON'T BE A FAN

Take emotions out of decision making.

"First rule of business is never get emotional about stock, clouds the judgment." - Michael Douglas (Gordon Gekko) in the movie Wall Street.

Wall Street is one of my favorite all-time movies. Sure, it was made in the late 80's and doesn't age well, especially if you look at the technology where Pac-Man looks like a futuristic game. But the lessons are timeless. It's all about the money, and the Sharps do whatever it takes to cash the tickets.

The sports world is a cruel world. In the NFL, most players are broke within 3 years of retiring. The professional leagues aren't concerned with the health of their players after their careers are over. The leagues get everything they can out of each player, and then kick them to the curb the moment they can't produce anymore. If a player can be replaced by a younger, cheaper replacement, it's done immediately without regard to who the person is. And that's how we need to treat sports gambling. We must treat every wager as if it means nothing emotionally. I can bet on a team one night, and against them the next night, and not blink any eye.

In sports gambling, controlling your emotions is one of the biggest and best attributes one can have. Every game is Team A vs.

Team B, not my favorite team against a team that I don't like. The book *Moneyball* by Michael Lewis taught us years ago to not get caught up in the emotional aspect of sports. Oakland A's General Manager Billy Beane got to a point where he didn't want to watch his team play, so that he could make unbiased roster decisions regarding his team. If we watch a baseball team 162 nights a year, it's easy to become emotionally attached to some guys, and not to others. And often, the numbers tell us that our gut instincts about players we like are completely wrong. How many people outside of San Francisco liked Barry Bonds in the late 90's and 2000's? Not many, but he was the best player in MLB according to WAR (Wins Above Replacement) from ages 35-39 in his career. Yet, I would play in numerous fantasy leagues and hear people say, "I'll never draft Bonds because he's on steroids!" Good! More money for me at the end of the season when I draft him and not blink an eye.

I've heard many fans of many teams say that they will either bet on their team, or not at all. In other words, they will never bet against their teams under any circumstances. When I was a kid, I liked certain teams. We all did it as kids. Sports can be very emotional and can bring out the best and worst emotions in anyone. But it should never affect your bankroll.

In Lexington, everybody loves the University of Kentucky. And when it comes to their basketball team, it's life and death in a lot of cases. But sometimes, the home team loses, as shocking as that is for some to believe. As a psychiatric study once, I listed the resumes and qualifications of Kentucky and archrival Tennessee on a paper and gave it to random people to see which team the good people of Lexington would pick to win the game. The trick was that I replaced the team names of Kentucky and Tennessee with Team A and Team B. No big deal, right?

An amazing thing happened! All these people were picking Team B! How can that be the case? Team B was the better team at every turn: KenPom rating, offense, defense, you name it! Team B was better. And every single person I asked picked Team B to win. Easy money, right?

But then I pulled back the curtains and told the hamsters the truth: Team A is Kentucky and Team B is Tennessee. Everyone reacted in one of two ways: either they laughed at how they consciously picked that horrible team from Tennessee to defeat their beloved Kentucky guys, or they immediately begged loudly to change from Team B to Team A. Wait a minute! The data hasn't changed! How can you change your choice from Team B to Team A? The only thing that changed is the perceived name on the front of the uniform. That is a sure sign of being a fan and being biased. For all the people that wanted to switch choices after the team names were revealed, they are fans. They are Squares. And they are unable to win at sports gambling long term.

I like to listen to other people's opinions about sports. Many people are much more informative and intelligent about sports than I am, so I always welcome a differing view. But even The Good Book says that we should be able to discern our information. "Don't cast your pearls before the swine," is another way of saying it. It means that we should be careful of who we listen to, because they aren't always the best sources of information. If I'm listening to a so-called "expert," whether it's in the media or associated to any sport, as soon as the "expert" refers to a team as "us," or "we," or "our," then I immediately check out. They are obviously biased, and following biased information is one of the quickest ways to lose in the desert. In Lexington, I often refer to the "Fan Boys Across Town." Those are the media members who do refer to the local Kentucky teams as "us," and would pick them to win against anyone in the history of sports. And that's OK, because the public eats that stuff up. The media who always pick the home teams get cheers, smiles, laughs, and the fans love them forever. While someone like me, who literally doesn't care who wins these games and will often pick against the local teams, gets called names and isn't as popular as the "Homers." It's just human nature.

When I first attempted to be a sports talk host in Lexington, I was able to do a few sound checks or sample shows to demonstrate what I could do behind the microphone. I just did a normal show that I would be doing if I had my own show. The first radio company that I interviewed with was very impressed with my work and they were ready to go forward with me. However, they wanted me to change 3 things about my topics: stop talking negatively about John Calipari (Kentucky basketball coach), stop talking negatively about Mark Stoops (Kentucky football coach), and stop talking so much about sports gambling and point spreads. Upon hearing this, I knew I was screwed! "That's all I have to change? That's all I've got! I've got three pitches, and that's it! I can't learn a knuckleball overnight." While most would think that was crazy, I knew I was telling the truth.

If I had gone on the radio, and yelled "Go Big Blue," for hours every day. I would fail miserably and immediately because I'm not a fan of the University of Kentucky sports teams. It's advantageous if they win because more people will listen to sports talk radio locally. And that means more people will listen to my show, and eventually/hopefully that means more money in my pocket. Unlike most fans, I get the same amount of sleep no matter what happens to the local teams in terms of winning or losing. I'm not out burning couches if they win, or throwing bricks through the television if they lose.

SIDE HUSTLE

Loyalty is something we all look for in our friends and family. It can mean the world to have people that you can depend on during bad times. And we ALL go through bad times at some point. But loyalty doesn't fly in the sports world. Have you seen how college athletics have changed in the last few years? Schools that were loyal to conferences one minute turn their back on those same conferences the next minute when someone flashes more money in their face. There is no loyalty in the sports world. And for fans of college or professional teams fall for that myth, that's when we make bad decisions. Professional franchises and universities have football teams to make money, and nothing else. It's a business, and it's a cruel business that will make fools of those who think otherwise.

I've also had people tell me, "I'll never listen to you again! It's like you don't even care if Kentucky wins or loses!" Unless I bet on them that night, you're right! I don't!

Another aspect of "don't be a fan" mentality is the sweat. Many beginning sports gamblers like to watch every game in which they have invested. As crazy as this sounds, I don't watch all the games. In fact, I don't watch many of the games at all. I can look at box scores and data to make better decisions than if I watch every game and become biased. Oakland A's General Manager Billy Beane didn't watch his team much during their run in the Moneyball era, and he seemed to do just fine making decisions based on being a contrarian, playing the game differently, and succeeding while doing things differently than the perceived Sharps like the Yankees and Red Sox of the day. When in reality, Beane was the Sharp, while the Yankees and Red Sox were the Squares. Beane was winning with less than half the bankroll to buy players, and yet could compete with them on the same level. That is the epitome of how we, as Squares, can compete against the Sharps. We can, but we must approach sports gambling differently than the Wise Guys in the Desert. Looking at data and box scores can be better than watching all the games, if that information is done properly and with discipline.

BOTTOM LINE

Sports are about making money, and nothing else. Franchises and schools don't care about the Squares. They just want your money. Sounds like sports books, right? Gordon Gekko told us to not get emotional over stock, and he was right. We don't have to sit up and sweat every single game we bet. But we can always take the information from those games in an unbiased manner and make a profit in the long term.

19
SELF-AWARENESS

Embrace your differences and do not try to be someone that you are not.

Keep your feet on the ground and keep reaching for the stars. - Casey Kasem.

True story: Casey Kasem, who was on radios for decades with his Top 40 Countdowns over the years, wanted to be a professional baseball player when he was growing up. I never saw that in him, but he figured out quickly that his voice would take him much farther than his ability to hit the curve ball. Kasem passed away in 2014, and he is STILL heard on the radio counting down the hits from the good old days. But at the end of his shows, he always said the quote above. And can help us sports gamblers keep some perspective. Having said that, don't get me started on those corny and lame Long Distance Dedications. Cut the cheese and get back to the hair bands, Kasem!

Here's the harsh truth. You're not going to get started in sports gambling and become one of the best in the world overnight. It takes decades of hurtful lessons and painful experience to do that.

Like me, Billy Walters (pictured above) grew up in Kentucky. Sadly, for my sports gambling abilities, that is where our similarities end. Walters is considered by many to be one of the best sports gamblers of all-time, if not THE best.

Billy Walters relied on information from sources. But how reliable are those sources? Chet Forte was the first director of Monday Night Football. But he was also an addicted gambler, which he kept on the down low out of sight from everyone else. On the day before the games, Forte and the Monday Night Football crew would sit with the coach and quarterback of the competing teams the following night. Forte got a lot of information and used it in bets. He listened to what these guys said, because nobody else was getting this information. He was an insider! Well, that information didn't help him. His gambling debts had been estimated to be $4 million. How can that be? He had just talked to the coaches and quarterbacks the day before. How could he lose? In fact, he would openly call in his bets in front of his co-workers on Monday Night Football. Just because we get what we think is inside information, it doesn't always mean we can profit from it. Do you think Bill Belichick is giving any information out to anyone before a Patriots game? If he does, he's just making stuff up.

Living in Atlanta the entire time he played for the Braves, Greg Maddux is probably my favorite baseball player of all-time. But the reasons have nothing to do with the fact that he played for the hometown team. I didn't really care if the Braves won or lost on a personal level, but I was a fan of cashing tickets. And few cashed tickets like Greg Maddux. He's a first ballot Hall of Famer, won both the Cy Young and the ERA title 4 times each, and won an incredible 18 Gold Gloves as the best fielding pitcher in MLB. He must have been a physical monster, right? Not at all! He wasn't a physcial specimen at all. Comparing him to the other great pitchers of his era wasn't even a comparison, as Maddux was lucky to get his fastball clocked more than 90 MPH. Yet, he had an ERA+ over 100 (meaning he was a "better than average" pitcher) 19 consecutive seasons. Sure, he cursed all the time. And yes, always threw the same cutter pitch to lefthanded hitters on the inside corner and he got 2 strikes on them. And yes, he benefitted from human umpires calling strike zones that would cause riots today (Go watch Game 5 of the 1997 NLCS for a blatant example). But he won the 8th most games in MLB history. And of the 7 players ahead of Maddux in career wins, the last year any of them took the field was 1965.

But what made Maddux so special? Why was he so good? He was smarter that the other pitchers. He prepared better than the other pitchers. And he never went into a game trying to strike out 20 and throw a perfect game. He just wanted to win the game. And as many games as Atlanta manager Bobby Cox blew for him with the Braves by taking him out after 7 innings and letting his pedestrian bullpen blow it was criminal. Maddux mastered fielding, with 18 Gold Gloves. In other words, he was different! In his time with the Braves, nobody managed him before or after games. He managed himself. He was the opposite of all the other great pitchers. And the most important thing about Maddux is that he didn't try to do things he couldn't do. He couldn't throw a 95+ MPH fastball. So he didn't try to do it.

Greg Maddux thought differently than everyone else. He was far from the most talented pitcher. Pedro Martinez and Randy Johnson were also great pitchers in his time, but they had far more physical talent than Maddux. Johnson was 6 feet 10 inches tall, with an incredible fastball and slider, and Martinez had "stuff" as good as anyone who ever played. They could strike out a dozen guys anytime they took the mound throughout almost their entire careers. Maddux relied on location, changing speed, and outthinking his opponents.

He loved being different than all the other great pitchers in his day. Knowing that he enjoyed that he was so different than the other pitchers, does it shock you that Maddux was born and raised in Las Vegas, Nevada? It shouldn't!

Do not try to be someone or something that you are not. If you think you are an NBA expert and bet the NBA games yet lose your tail because you do not have the time or hustle to keep up with the Load Management stuff every day, then you are not an NBA expert. Wait until the playoffs like I do. I used to bet NBA regular season games. But when Load Management started, and I had to hustle more to get the information on who was playing or not playing in each game, I packed up the bags and said, "Smell Ya Later" to NBA wagering until the playoffs. I know in the playoffs that everyone who can play is playing. I do not know that in the regular season, and I do not have the time to do all the homework for every game. I was able to look in the mirror and see that I could no longer feasibly bet the NBA anymore until the Spring.

Having said all this, I can never be Billy Walters. And honestly, you can never be Billy Walters. How he moved lines is something that very few can ever do. Trust me when I tell you, the oddsmakers do not move lines based on our Pizza Money bets. In other words, we cannot be Billy Walters. So, let's not try to be Billy Walters. Phil Mickelson might be around the corner ready to sabotage your entire life, and then smile like nothing happened.

BOTTOM LINE

I cannot be as good of a sports gambler as Billy Walters, and I'm not trying to be like that. I can't do what he does. I'm trying to be as good as Brad Taylor, a guy who is happy to grind out 53% winners in a good year. It's always a good idea to get tips from the best in any business. But at the end of the day, you can only do what fits your life best. You can't go send bet runners out to make big bets and change lines, then go the other way. You are like me, just trying to pick enough winners to make a profit. Casey Kasem had it right: Keep your feet on the ground but keep reaching for the stars. Look to play sports gambling your **Side Hustle**, but don't think you can change the world by winning all your bets. You can't.

20

TRAPS

The oddsmakers don't make mistakes.

"Things That Make You Go Hmmm..." - C&C Music Factory.

Another R&B group from back in the day. They tried to out-Milli Vanilli the original Milli Vanilli as Martha Wash sang the vocals on C&C's biggest hits but didn't front the band or appear in their videos. Image was everything back then, and still is if you want to be honest. Although not their biggest hit, their most quoted hit was *"Things That Make You Go Hmmm..."* It was a staple of the Arsenio Hall show, a personal favorite from those days. And I still think of it today.

Sports gamblers are conditioned to think that oddsmakers make mistakes. News flash: they don't! When you see a line that doesn't make sense, or doesn't agree with your ratings or eye test, it's because the desert knows things that you don't know. And anytime you see a line that makes no sense at all, you should pay attention to what the desert is trying to tell you.

A great time to look out for these "traps" is in college football and basketball. The AP Poll is something the Squares look at as a handicapping tool. The Sharps look at it as something to go completely against. There are several occasions throughout the college football and basketball seasons where you will see a team ranked in the AP Top 25 poll an underdog to an unranked opponent. How can that be? The pollsters know it all! Squares will sprint to the window with fists full of hundreds to get on that ranked team because the oddsmakers made a mistake. No, they didn't. Anytime you see this, and you'll see it almost daily during college basketball conference season, look to take the unranked favorite. The desert is telling you who the better team is. Listen to them! They're smarter than we are!

That goes for professional point spread leagues as well, especially the NFL. Ever see a game where one team is decidedly better so far in the season than the other team, yet the line is far less than you'd expect? Again, if the desert is telling you something, listen. There's a reason every line is where it is. And unlike what the old school commercials used to tell you, the oddsmakers don't make mistakes that could cost them a lot of money.

The teams that should be favored, are favored. The teams that should be underdogs, are underdogs. The underdogs have more value, but the point here is that the oddsmakers in the desert don't make mistakes! When sports gambling touts still advertised on the radio years ago, one of the sales pitches was "The oddsmakers have made a mistake! Call 1-900-whatever to find out where the desert is wrong!" To think that some people called that number after hearing that still amazes me to this day. There's too much money on the line for the oddsmakers to make mistakes.

BOTTOM LINE

Regardless of what you think you know, the oddsmakers in the desert know even more. They have better information than you. Sorry to burst your bubble. When you see an unranked team favored over a ranked team, look to take the unranked favorite. Always look to follow the oddsmakers when a line doesn't agree with conventional wisdom. There's a reason why the line is what it is. Don't fall for the trap!

21
THE PROLINE EFFECT

Don't pay for picks

"The less you bet, the more you lose, when you win." - Kelso Sturgeon, former handicapper, panelist on the old ProLine show.

One of my favorite shows to watch back in the 80's and 90's was ProLine. It was usually on the USA Network very early Saturday mornings. And by "very early" we are talking 6:00 AM. It was basically an infomercial for the gambling "touts" to promote their 1-900 phone numbers (back in the day, we had 1-900 phone numbers that cost a varying amount per call or minute of phone call. Google it, kids!). And for differing dollar amounts, you get the knowledge from the horse's mouth you heard on TV earlier that morning. For X amount of dollars, you can get 3, 5, heck, why not a dozen guaranteed "10,000-star, Super-Galactic Locks of the Millennium." And those picks were guaranteed, or you play the rest of the season for free! I loved watching that show. Not as much for the football knowledge dropped, of which there was very little, but for the promos for the 1-900 numbers. Some would claim to be hitting over 90% winners for that season, and you are missing out on the deal of a lifetime without the free money they are giving away.

That quote from Kelso Sturgeon might not make any sense the first time you read it but give it a minute. Although it's a true statement, in theory, this is nothing more than a way to get us Squares to bet more (and potentially lose more).

But don't be mistaken! ProLine was a masterpiece of television history. It was one of the greatest shows of all time! I loved this show! Not because I was going to bet on their picks and waste hundreds of dollars by calling them, but because I felt like eventually, I could handicap sporting events as a **Side Hustle** and just wanted to hear the jargon from those who allegedly could.

So why did I like this show? Even at a young age, I could tell these guys were almost like used car salesmen. The former coach who's been in the locker rooms while hitting 95% winners for the season, the "insider" who knows the inside information nobody else does while hitting 96% on the season, and the computer "nerd" that can tell you about the exact necessary trajectory on a 38-yard field goal attempt from the right hash and picks (you guessed it) 97% winners. They had everything that appealed to the prospective sports gambler except one thing: actual winners.

A friend of mine asked me once decades ago if he should call one of these tout services. I asked him how much the phone call was, and he said $50. I asked him how much he was going to bet, and he then slowly said $50, as if he realized the math all at once. Conversation over.

Paying for picks also means 52.38% is gone. If you pay for your picks, you must hit more than 52.38%. Those touts might tell you that they hit 95% but pay for their picks and see for yourself how many they hit. They might come up just a little bit short.

And since sports gambling has expanded outside of the state of Nevada, these touts are everywhere now! But here's something I've noticed on social media quite a bit: I see all kinds of people talking about their winning tickets and posting pictures of them AFTER the fact. How about people posting their tickets BEFORE the games are played? That's how things should be done, but in this sports gambling world, nobody likes a loser. And to most people, only picking 53% winners is a loser. After reading this book, we all know 53% winners can get us that yacht out on the ocean.

BOTTOM LINE

If you're going to lose, lose on your own. Don't pay some tout to give you losers when you can do that just fine for yourself. Create your own **Side Hustle** by doing your homework, focusing on underdogs, road teams, under totals, and going against the public. You'll be just as good, and probably better, than these touts who are trying to get money for nothing and chicks for free.

22
POSITIVE REINFORCEMENT

Environment matters

"He's gone! You lose! You lose, Brad!" - a friend who was delighted I was about to lose my bet as Warrick Dunn scored against Florida in 1993.

The college football season of 1993 was wild. Florida State was the best team, but they truly were fortunate to finally win the school a national championship. For that matter, 1993 was a wild time, as we were still stuck in the pre-internet world that would shortly change, but not soon enough for this day.

It was November of 1993. I was home for the Thanksgiving holiday in Kentucky. And on a Saturday afternoon, a couple of friends and I were watching college football. Florida and Florida State were playing, with the Gators a 3.5-point home underdog to mighty #1 ranked FSU. If you've been paying attention in this book, you won't be shocked to learn that I took Florida as the home dog. My other friends with me at the time also took Florida. As the game neared its conclusion, another friend stops by and joins us. He's also a big football fan, but he's jealous that he didn't get any action down on this game while the rest of us did. "Thanks for including me, losers!" He's showing his "taking my ball and going home" mentality at this point. Since he's the only person in the room who doesn't have a bet on the game, he starts openly rooting against us. But for some reason, he blames me more than the others that I didn't ask him if he wanted to bet on the game. I'm just visiting for the holiday week, yet I'm supposed to oversee these things. Ridiculous! This was in the age before cell phones and texting. We just played everything by ear back in those prehistoric days.

Anyway, the game is in the 4th quarter and Florida is down by 6. All they need to do is stop Florida State on this big 3rd downplay with a little over 5 minutes to go, get the ball and score, and we cash another ticket. Florida State had other ideas as Heisman Trophy winner Charlie Ward hit Warrick Dunn with an 80-yard touchdown pass (pictured above) to win the game and cash the ticket for Florida State. Oh well, we lost. Let's move on to the next game. But wait a minute, our jealous friend is too busy jumping up and down with joy! As Dunn caught the pass and broke free before he reached midfield, my friend stood up and yelled, "He's gone! You lose! You lose, Brad!" And he did it with such joy in his heart, with a big smile on his face. After the shock of the game winning play wore off and the television coverage went to commercial, I immediately turned to my friend and asked, "What did you say while that play was going on?" He started to laugh hysterically, knowing he had been busted for openly rooting against me because I had action on the game, and he didn't. In fact, we were all laughing because it was so stupid. For years after that, when I would see him, I would eventually yell, "He's gone! You lose, Brad!" It's easy for us to laugh about now, and it was easy to laugh about then as well. But for a few seconds it was someone revealing their true emotions.

When I was a kid going to The Red Mile racetrack in Lexington, Kentucky, I would see this among those people as well. It was a competition between each other to see who could win and who would lose. Some people even got mad if you picked the same horse as they did, even if you both won! In spots like these, we are competing against the house, not each other. Sometimes, when I went to the Red Mile with people I knew, I would write down some quotes of some of the ridiculous things I heard from the evening's festivities. Quotes about gambling, insulting each other, hoping the other person loses their tail, etc. The mean-spirited insults and clichés were seen as normal at the time and had little reaction from other people. But later, we would read those quotes when the night of racing was over, and they became hysterical of how crazy everyone behaved while just trying to cash some tickets. It's amazing what gambling can do to a person who hasn't been around the block a few times.

Earlier, I talked about "Envelope Games." Those are bets among friends who are in the same room and will watch the game together. But since nobody trusted anybody in those spots back in the day when we were all fighting over pennies, we would put our money in an envelope before the game and set it on the table so that the loser couldn't make up excuses to why they couldn't pay immediately after the result was known. Those are the types of things that speak volumes about the people you're rolling with, although it does provide for high comedy.

I've become a much better handicapper since I've just been doing this on my own without watching games with other people. In fact, doing it this way causes a lot less stress. Sometimes we must mentally rise above the haters that want to see us lose just as much as they want to win themselves, which is a concept I can't wrap my arms around but it's out there. When you're in a social situation with people like this, it can sometimes affect you in the way you handicap games. And that's Square thinking! If the people you are with change how you handicap games for whatever reason, it's time for a change.

BOTTOM LINE

Surround yourself with people who are supportive of your sports betting. There will always be negative people who think they can do it better than you. And there will always be people jealous that they can't get the action down that you can. It's funny among friends to wish them nothing but bad luck and openly root for them to lose. But at the end of the day, this is real money we are talking about here. This isn't for slaps and tickles. It's one thing if I put a curse on Bo Jackson while playing Tecmo Bowl so you'll stop running that darn sweep to the bottom of the screen on every single play. It's another thing if you put a curse on me and I've got a few bills on the line. Get a feel for the room and the moment.

23
LIGHTNING ROUND

The Basics

"This week, we are getting back to basics." - Any coach whose team is on a losing streak.

Have you ever heard a coach or a team on a winning streak claim they need to get "back to basics?" Not a chance! Usually, this is the cry from a team that started well, then hit a losing streak, and wants things to get back to the way they were.

Sports gambling can be very similar. A gambler can start off hot, then hit a cold streak, and try to make things like they were when he was hot. Odds are, the gambler who started hot probably increased his/her bet size as well, a sure-fire plan for failure. The key is not to change things! Keep doing the same type of handicapping. Bad streaks happen, just weather the storm!

As a kid growing up, my little world revolved around game shows on television. Both my parents were out hustlin', and once I got too old for Sesame Street, it was game shows. In fact, my secret goal in life when I was very young was to be a game show host. Just don't tell anyone. It's kind of lame, and I can assure you I don't have that Game Show Hair that is a mandatory pre-requisite.

Many game shows had something called "The Lightning Round," as a bonus to the winners. In fact, the last couple of minutes of my radio show always ends in a segment called, "What did we learn on The **Bottom Line** today?" And then I tell a bunch of silly lies and end the show. In that spirit, here is the Lightning Round of Sports Gambling Basics.

Look to take mostly underdogs and going under totals. History tells us that it is better than taking favorites and over totals.

Take emotions out of your decision-making process.

Winning sports bettors look treat this as a marathon, not a sprint.

Any bet with a juice/vig of more than –110 is not your friend.

Shoot to win 100% of your bets, but be thrilled with 53%

Open plenty of accounts, taking advantage of signup bonuses, so you can shop around for the best lines.

Don't bet out of your comfort zone. One bet should never change your life.

Trust the numbers and the data more than your biased eye test.

BOTTOM LINE

Following these basic Lightning Round tips will put you ahead of plenty of Squares. Now, let's try to compete with the Sharps and pick some winners.....

PART II

LET'S MAKE SOME MONEY!

SIDE HUSTLE

SIDE HUSTLE

THE PRE-GAME PLAN

"If You Fail to Plan, You Are Planning to Fail" — *Benjamin Franklin*

Winston Churchhill, one of the greatest examples of not giving up in history, used this quote. John Wooden, the biggest winner in college basketball history, used this quote. But Ben Franklin is credited with being the first to coin this line. Ironically, Ben Franklin is also the face on the $100 bill, the one thing we are trying to get our grubby hands on by picking winners. Coincidence? I think not! I had a teacher tell me this once. He also threatened to "sink me like a 3-foot putt." Obviously, I chalked it up as being the usual crazy talk from someone who hadn't experienced life in the real world, but he was actually right about this one! We have to plan ahead before we can become a successful sports gambler.

But how do we plan ahead to be a Sharp before we place a bet? Here are some good things to have set before you start:

BANKROLL

I'm a very firm believer that sports gambling is a marathon, not a sprint. And in saying that, your beginning bankroll reflects how a sports gambler is going into this.

Keep in mind, that your bankroll to start should be an amount that you can comfortably lose. In other words, whatever amount of money that you have when you begin, just plan on losing every penny of it. Odds are that you will, unless you play this correctly.

I am also of the belief that one bet shouldn't change your life. We will get to this when we talk about parlay bets, which are Fool's Gold. But why do you think the casinos leak to the media that someone hit a ridiculous 10-team parlay and put up $10 to win $125,000? The sports books want to give the sports bettors a mustard seed's worth of hope that they can do the same thing. When in reality, it's almost like hitting the lottery. If you are playing this long term, one bet shouldn't change your life whatsoever. But hitting 53% winners long term will. The best sports bettors in the world don't play huge multi-team parlays on a consistent basis. Just like you don't see someone driving a Mercedes lining up to buy scratch off lottery tickets. It's the same mentality.

I never bet more than 5% of my bankroll on a single wager. In fact, I actually will only bet 1% of my bankroll. It seems low and conservative, but I never have to worry about bankrolls shrinking to where I can't play anymore. I had someone ask me how much they should bet per wager if they started with $1,000 in their accounts. I replied that I would only be wagering $10 per game with that amount of money. That answer didn't make him happy when I told him. "I've got $1,000, and I'm only supposed to bet $10 per game? That's ridiculous! I was thinking maybe $100 per bet" Maybe it is ridiculous! But if that guy starts out 4-6 in his first 10 wagers at $100 each, he's already down to 74% of his original $1,000 bankroll. But if he bet 1% of his bankroll, he still has 97.4%. The "no risk, no reward" people are screaming right now, but those are true gamblers who often only have hope on their sides. While we are trying to grind out a profit long term. It's a big difference. If you want to play this long term, save more money for your initial bankroll. It's that simple.

Sports gambling isn't a steady increase of money. There are ups and downs, ebbs and flows, hot streaks and cold streaks. Can you survive the tough times burning 10% of your bankroll per wager? Not a chance. Can you survive with only 1% wagers? You have a MUCH better chance. My reply to my friend who wanted to bet more per game with the $1,000 bankroll was, "Hey, if you want to bet more and survive, then save more money before you start!"

When beginning your sports gambling journey, make sure to save enough money for your opening bankroll that you can COMFORTABLY lose where it doesn't affect you financially or mentally. Only you can answer that question of how much is too much because we are all different. But beginning sports gamblers start slow until they experience the joys of winning, and more importantly, the heartaches of losing.

PREPARING OTHERS

If you're like me, you deal with people throughout most days. Whether it's family, friends, co-workers, or whatever, there's people in this world who want your time. Finding your own time around them is key, without letting it affect you or them.

The best thing we as sports gamblers can do is share with them that you need the time to handicap games. Don't hide the fact that you are trying to make some money with sports gambling as your new Side Hustle. Be honest and tell them. That way, they will hopefully try to help you instead of assuming the worst of how you're spending time on your computer in private! Most people will originally look at you like you're crazy when you intially share this with them, and some will dismiss you as an addicted gambler who is now on the Dark Side of life because you're putting sports gambling in front of them. But you're not! We all have hobbies, whether it's selling stuff on eBay, or watching television, or our pets, or whatever. We all have things we enjoy doing outside of our careers, and sometimes away from loved ones. It's OK. If those people care about you and what you want to do, tell them what you're doing. If they are worth their salt, they will give you the time and space necessary to allow you the room to possibly make a profit at sports gambling.

And this brings me to another aspect of sports gambling and those who surround you. Make sure that the people who are closest to you have no idea if you're on a hot streak or a cold streak. In other works, do your best to keep that Lady Gaga-like Poker Face. If you are one of those people that wears your emotions on your sleeve, and losing a bet can ruin your entire week, this might not be the gig for you. As I've gotten older, it's become much easier to not allow losing sports wagers to ruin my day, because they don't! The people close to me can't tell if I've won or lost a fortune in the last 72 hours. Once you can pull that off, you're ahead of the game. Because the last thing we as sports gamblers want to do, is let losing affect other people in a negative way.

TIME AND ROUTINE

This might be my most difficult part of being a successful sports gambler. Finding time and getting the routine down.

There are certain days of the week when I have more responsibilities than others. On Thursdays, my day is very hectic. I'm several different places, taking care of all kinds of people and matters, both work-related and family related. It can be a crazy day! It also has an effect on my handicapping results. I am a stickler for keeping results of my sports wagering. What sports am I best and worst at handicapping on a weekly basis? In the past, Thursday was my worst day of the week! Shocking that it also happened to be my most hectic day of the week as well, isn't it? I made changes in my schedule to give me more time to handicap games, and my performance improved.

We have to give ourselves enough time to get our handicapping finished on a daily basis. That means making time. But how do we do that when we have a job, and family, and people who need our time? You have to make the time. Or else, you will get behind like I did on Thursdays when I had lots of responsibilities. If it's your lunch hour at work, or spending time after work before you go home, or even early morning, you have to make time to handicap games. And it's not just looking at lines and guessing based on hunches and eye tests. It's data-driven handicapping of games.

SIGNING UP

There's plenty of sports books that will be happy to take your money these days. And they will give you bonuses for just showing up in the first place.

Although "brick and mortar" sports books still exist, over 98% of bets come in through phone apps. Each app determines where you are via GPS to determine whether you are in a legal state that has passed sports betting laws and makes it as easy as sending a text to a friend to bet your life away. The books are so confident that you will lose, that they offer huge sign-up bonuses to new customers. The books are saying, "Sure, we will double what you give us initially, because we know you're going to lose! Come on in! The water's fine!" Little do they know that after reading this book, you will have a much better chance of turning that bonus into a big profit than they think.

But make sure to get as many accounts as you can to start, and cash in on those sign-up bonuses too! Take what the game gives you! The more accounts you have, the better chance you have of winning! If you want to take a team that's a 6-point underdog most places, but one of your accounts has that same team as a 6.5-point dog, which account will you use? Yes! The 6.5-point line! A Square might think there's no difference in just a half point here or there. But believe me, over time, it's a HUGE difference. That's why signing up with as many sports books can be very profitable. It can make the difference between a 52% winner (actually a loser), and a 53% winner (turning a profit).

KEEP TRACK OF BETS

It's extremely important to keep track of your bets, and not just look at your account balances the next day. Keep track of how you are doing in each sport. But also keep track of how you do in certain situations: sport, day of week, location of handicapping. All these seem like silly things, but they are far from it. There's one day each week where I have more to do than the others, and I didn't handicap games nearly as well on that day for a while. I noticed it by keeping track of my bets. I was able to change some things and become a better handicapper on my busy day of the week.

LEARNING FROM MISTAKES

Sports gamblers should take note of the story of Winston Churchill. This was a man who lost, and lost big, so many times in his career. He lost several elections, put his British people into great turmoil with his decisions, and spent 10 years in hiding after humiliating himself publicly. But just when everyone had given up on Churchill many times, he continued his risk-taking behavior and became one of the most celebrated people, much less politicians, in the British history. He never lost his confidence in what he was doing, and continued to do what he knew would work. But it was a long and winding road to get there, and there can be collateral damage to those who don't persevere.

Play to your strengths! Put your bankroll into the sports you have historically done the best in wagering. If you enjoy wagering on certain sports, but aren't very successful in doing so, it's a good idea to limit your bets and wagering on them. Making bets for entertainment value only is nice, but it's also another way to lose money. It's fine to play a few sports, and even a few conferences or divisions in those sports, if that's what your history says works for you. And you'll only learn that from looking at your mistakes.

SIDE HUSTLE

RECOGNIZING WINNERS

THE STOCK MARKET

At some time during every season, a team's stock is overvalued or undervalued. Buy low, sell high. It works in the stock market, and it works in sports gambling. If a team is losing, look to bet them.

Raiders of the Lost Cause. Give us your tired, your poor, your weak. These teams are very undervalued. The world loves the winners, and the women love them too. Take teams nobody trusts. Teams that lose a few games to start the season, people are late to come around because it takes a while for people to catch up.

BETTING THE BOARD?

Bet a lot of games? Or quality/quantity? I know I can go 9 out of 16 on an NFL weekend, right? A lot of people feel like they MUCH bet Monday night football because it's a national television game, it's the only NFL game of the day, and they need the action after a big Sunday. It's a recipe for disaster to bet every game on the board, or to feel like you must bet a game because it's a stand-alone weeknight game. Lem Banker, the late great sports gambler himself, once said, "They play the national anthem every day." In other words, you don't have to bet every game. Hype of commercials. That's their job! When I first started playing fantasy football in 1990, I was reading a book about strategies on making player decisions. This book told me

"When in doubt, play the guy on Monday night so you can watch him for yourself." Talk about Square thinking!

Monday Night Football has always been about gambling. And now, so is Thursday and Sunday Night Football. Stand-alone games that the entire sports gambling world sees and bets. Doubling up on Monday Night Football after a big weekend as you're playing with "house money" doesn't work. That "house money" you've won has probably come after giving the house a lot of your money in the past. You're just finally getting some back. 99 out of 100 sports gamblers lose money on football. If you win on Sunday, walk away happy. Then bet the same amount on Monday's game that you did on Sunday.

You ever wonder why your old school bookie around the corner collects to Tuesday/Wednesday? Because they knew people were desperate on Monday night, and people were ready to let it ride. Don't make a bigger bet on Monday Night Football than any other game. The game has the same value as the Sunday at 1:00 Jaguars/Colts game. And for that matter, the same value the Reds/Cubs game played in anonymity on a September Sunday afternoon when everyone else is watching football.

DEFENSE > OFFENSE

Defense wins championships. Offense burns tickets. History always repeats itself. If you don't study history you are doomed to fail. Some teams break out of the gates in a season by putting up a ton of points, and the public loves them, Patrick Mahomes comes to mind. Then like clockwork, and then suddenly they face a boring team with a good defense and a mediocre QB and that team usually takes down the high-flying offensive team. Maybe not straight up, but where it counts for us: against the spread. Always look for defensive oriented teams, because they are always undervalued in the desert. At the same time, the public loves the teams that put up the big numbers on offense, and those teams are overvalued.

"Nobody goes there anymore, it's too crowded." - Yogi Berra

SIDE HUSTLE

THE FALLACY OF 52.38%

Why isn't this number what we are told it is?

We are told that to break even in the desert we need to hit 52.38% of our bets. That is true, but only if you follow certain criteria that very few bettors follow consistently.

To break even at 52.38% a bettor must do the following:
- Bet the same amount on every wager.
- Pay a juice/vig of –110 for every wager.

Then, and ONLY then, does the 52.38% winning percentage mean that a bettor breaks even. But how often does that happen? VERY rarely. Bettors unwisely increase/decrease their wager amounts all the time. And bettors with only one betting account are often stuck with –115 or –120 juice/vig on some bets.

Oh, stop whining **Side Hustle** Guy. -115 isn't going to kill you. It's not? Here's what a bettor must do to break even when paying bigger juice/vig than –110

Juice/Vig   -110   **% of winners to break even**: 52.38%
Juice/Vig   -115   **% of winners to break even**: 53.49%
Juice/Vig   -120   **% of winners to break even**: 54.55%

This is difficult enough at 52.38%. Now I have to lay juice and win almost 55% of the time at -120? No way! Have enough accounts where you won't have to lay more than –110 juice/vig. Laying anything more than that is just a recipe for losing long term.

SIDE HUSTLE

LET'S MAKE SOME BETS!

POINT SPREADS BETS

Here we go! The main method of sports betting.

Team A −4.5

Team B

In this case, Team A is a 4-and-a-half-point favorite over Team B. The "minus" sign means that team is favored by the number of points after the minus sign. Team B is +4.5, which means that they are the underdog.

For Team A to cash your ticket, they must win the game by more than 4.5 points (5 or more). For Team B to cash your ticket, Team B must win the game, or lose by less than 4.5 points (4 or less).

If the line was Team A −5, and the game finished with Team A winning by 5, the game would be a "push" and all tickets would be refunded. One of our −110 bets that we like to play.

MONEYLINE BETS

"You play to win the game!" - Former NFL player and coach Herm Edwards

Money line bets are exactly what Herm said: it's just picking the winners. However, the −110 juice/vig is out the window on these. Here is a typical money line:

Team A −150

Team B +130

SIDE HUSTLE

Used more often in MLB than any of the major sports, the money line bet is simply betting the team that wins the game.

Money lines are listed based on winning $100 for a wager. If you want to win $100 by betting Team A, the bettor would have to bet $150 to get back his original $150 and his $100 winnings. If a bettor placed $100 on Team B, a Team B win would reward him with his $100 wager and $130 in winnings. Playing money line takes the 52.38% completely out of play but can be profitable by playing short underdogs.

TOTALS

Team A
Team B   Total 48.5

Totals are the points scored for the game between the two teams. For the game above to go over the total, Team A and Team B would need to combine for 49 or more points as a final score. To go under the total, the final score must be 48 or less. Another good −110 bet.

PROP BETS

Will Player A score a touchdown tonight? Will Starting Pitcher B strike out more or fewer than 5.5 batters during his start? Props bets are very popular, especially with new bettors. And they can be profitable if played conservatively. The biggest problem with Prop Bets is the juice/vig. Unlike our side and total bets which are usually −110, a bettor will often have to lay quite a bit of juice on these Prop Bets. Keep this in mind when factoring them into your long-term bankroll. Even though they look tempting, laying −130 or more juice makes them almost must wins to earn a profit long-term. The juice is the key for Prop Bets. Don't look to lay more than −110. Unfortunately, this rules out a lot of Prop Bets.

SIDE HUSTLE

FUTURES

Futures are an entire breed to themselves. Future Bets are very long-term. Which team will win their division, conference, or national/world championship. The desert rarely gives you full value on season long Future Bets.

Many bettors also like to bet on Futures in awards. Who will win the MVP, Rookie of the Year, Comeback Player of the Year, etc. Keep in mind when betting these awards that the human element is involved in voting. In the 2022-23 NBA Season, Nikola Jokic was better than Joel Embiid. This was proven both in the regular season, and in the playoffs. But Jokic had won the previous 2 MVP awards, and voters get tired of giving the MVP to the same guy every year. Want proof? Michael Jordan won the MVP award 5 times. He was the best player in the league for a lot more than 5 seasons. Voters are fickle. Keep that in mind when betting Futures that come down to humans voting.

1st HALF/2nd HALF and FIRST 5 INNINGS

Along with betting full games, bettors can only bet quarters or halves of games if they are so inclined. Personally, I look to starting pitchers now as First 5 Inning wagers due to bullpen usage making them less of a handicapping tool for a 9-inning game.

Halftime is a good time to look for value in 2nd half lines, especially in games in which one team has a big lead. Alabama football under Nick Saban is notorious for piling up a huge halftime lead, then coasting home. If a game line was Team A –5 before the game, and Team A is up by 15 at halftime, looking to take Team B in the 2nd half.

Books will often raise the juice/vig on these 1st/2nd half wagers as well, so make sure the juice doesn't eat up your bankroll.

PARLAYS AND TEASERS

How can I put this: DON'T DO PARLAYS! And teasers aren't far behind! The following is all you need to know about parlays:

UNLV did a 40-year study of all Nevada Sportsbooks. They found the following:

- House profits 30% on all parlay wagers
- House profits 5% on all other sportsbook wagers.

If you can argue with that, then good luck. Have you ever wondered why the media makes a big deal out of Bettor A who won a 10-team parlay and cashed a $150k ticket? The books feed this information to the media, who runs with it for content. They're trying to give some hope to people who are looking for that one big hit. News flash: it's probably not happening to you!

The Stanford Wong NFL teaser was a great system back in the day. Tease home teams that were favorites of 7.5 to 8.5. Tease all teams that are 1.5 to 2.5 dogs. It got teams through the magical NFL numbers of 3 and 7. Easy money, right? It was easy money when the juice/vig was what it used to be. Sadly, the desert caught up to this. Now, most places that 6-point teaser will cost you –120 juice/vig. Do you want to pay for that? I don't! Most places have priced themselves out of the Stanford Wong teaser business. But if you can find –110 or less, it's still a good play. Otherwise, parlays and teasers are for the Squares, not the Sharps.

SIDE HUSTLE

IN-GAME WAGERS

Here's the new fad: betting sporting events during live action. These are especially the rage in golf at the present time. In the major sports, I like to wait until a timeout or a break in the action for live in-game wagers, and there are algorithms that make a lot of these lines that the Sharps that are watching the games live can take advantage of on a regular basis. Again, the juice/vig can sometimes get out of hand, so keep an eye out for these. Watching games toward end of halves and being able to read which team will have the ball last (football and basketball) can give a first half wagerer a competitive advantage, but it takes hustle to make this a Side Hustle.

SIDE HUSTLE

LOOK FOR MARKET SIGNS

BETTING SPLITS: Looking for the Sharp Money

We hear all the time now the Squares are on one side, and the Sharps are on the other. How can we identify these instances? Squares are tickets, and Sharps are money. Look for a web site that will provide Bet Splits. If one team has more tickets on them to cover a point spread, but the other team has more money on them to cover the spread, the team with the most money is the Sharp side. The Sharp side has more high roller bets from professional bettors, while the Square side has amateur bettors looking to just get minimal money on their favorite teams. Anytime you see 15% more money than tickets on one side, that is a sure-fire indicator of the Sharp side.

REVERSE LINE MOVE: How did that happen?

Another mysterious way to play the market is to look for Reverse Line Moves (RLM). This is a spot where the money is one side, but the line is moving to the other side. That doesn't make sense, does it? How is all the money going here, but the line is moving there? That's Sharp money once again dictating the market. And I'd rather be with the Sharps than the Squares.

STEAM MOVE: Let it out quickly!

Steam is a sudden line movement on a game across most sportsbooks. It is generally the result of a wave of money coming on a single side of a game from a betting syndicate or large sharp bettors. It's better to be ahead of the steam than behind it.

Chasing Steam is a strategy where a bettor can move quickly to get down a wager at a slower sportsbook that has yet to change their line with the rest of the market. Look for slower Square books to pull off these tricks of the trade.

TRAPS: Beware!

In college football or basketball, when you see an unranked team favored over a ranked team, look to take the favored unranked team. I rarely suggest taking favorites in point spread wagers, but here's an occasion where I will look for information why I should NOT lay the favorite in this spot. The desert is telling you that they know more than the AP pollsters, and they do. The Squares don't believe that. The Sharps know it as fact.

TRENDS AND SYSTEMS

"Trends don't pay the mortgage." - Jimmy Vaccaro.

"Trends don't pay the mortgage, but systems implemented the right way can pay the utility bills." - Brad Taylor.

Jimmy Vaccaro is royalty in the sports gambling world. If he says something related to sports gambling, we should all pay attention and heed his words. That's Sharps and Squares alike!

But who are we to question the great Jimmy Vaccaro? He has seen more tickets cashed and more tickets burned than we could in dozens of lifetimes as quite possibly the most legendary oddsmaker in the history of the desert. Anything this man says regarding sports gambling should be listened to astutely and taken into heavy consideration. But a system is different than a trend. This is what Vaccaro was talking about when he said that trends couldn't pay the mortgage.

Trends are given out all the time. On my radio show, I use trends at times as fodder or material that will get the listener to think, or to back up a point I'm trying to make. "Team A is 9-3 against the spread in their last 12 games." To be honest, that is actually more information to go against Team A than to go on Team A. New or rookie sports bettors rely on small and short trends way too much. If it happened 5 out of 7 times, it would happen again! It also brings a built-in excuse if they lose! And when the media uses these trends with no firm basis for success, many use it to sounds like they know what they're talking about. But in reality, the media knows just as much – if not less than – picking winners in the desert as anyone reading this book.

The System was a musical act back in the 80's that had a song called, "Don't Disturb This Groove." I have that cassette tape somewhere in my library of shoeboxes full of 80's music. But their song is an ironic name for this book because we can use it for getting a daily routine, and definitely for using systems. When a sports gambler gets into a groove using successful systems, the profits can start to slowly accumulate. The key word in that sentence is "slowly." Once again, just because a system has worked for decades, that doesn't mean it will win for you immediately. We are in this for the long haul. If you use a system for 3 weeks, take some losses, then give up on it, that's the recipe for losers with no patience. And believe me when I tell you, playing these systems I describe in this book is the long play over long periods of time. If you don't have the patience for it, you'll lose. It's plain and simple.

But there's a difference between trends and systems. Trends are recent, hence the off-putting term in sports gambling we sometimes use "Recency Bias." A system has been proven over very long periods of time with huge amounts of sample size data from which to pick.

Here's a little trick the media likes to play on us to get us thinking the wrong way. If a team has won 4 of their last 5, they have really won 4 of their last 6. The media takes numbers like these and exaggerates them to make them sound better than they really are. 4 out of 5 is 80%, while 4 out of 6 is 67%. It may not seem like much, but over time it makes a difference.

The biggest difference between trends and systems are sample size. If I hear of Team A has covered the spread 8 out of 10 times in a certain scenario, that means nothing to me. The magic number for me is at least 50 games. Even 50 games as a minimum sample size is a little light, but at least with 50 we have some solid results with which to work. The larger the sample size data we are working with, the better the system is if it is a proven winner over time. In this book, we will review systems with well over 10,000 games over more than 2 decades that will prove out points. And working with systems that have larger sample sizes takes the Recency Bias factor out of things even more.

Another pitfall for new sports bettors is falling for Recency Bias. There's a reason The Zig Zag Theory, an NBA system by simply taking the team that lost the last game in the next game, was so successful for so many years before the oddsmakers adapted. Only the sharps had the guts to ignore what happened in the last game and go the opposite way. Unlike Diamonds and The Four Horsemen, streaks don't last forever. Janet Jackson asked is in the past, "what have you done for me lately?" Good song (without the wardrobe malfunction, which was completely contrived), but she probably wasn't a salty sports gambler like us. "Lately" aren't a few weeks with less than 50 games of data. It's 20 years of data with tried-and-true systems that have made profits.

As sports bettors, we are in this for the long term. Just like these teams, we as sports gamblers also endure hot and cold streaks throughout the season. The systems I use have been cultivated over many years, and hundreds (sometimes thousands) or sample size data. A trend that has won 8 of 10 doesn't mean a whole lot when we are looking at a couple of decades of data. And with recent trends, the desert is also on to these that the media pushes. The odds have already factored in the public jumping on these trends. MLB teams on a winning streak are paying a higher price than if they had won 5 out of 10, for example. Squares act on the recent past. Sharps act on historical data. This is one of many reasons why Sharps win more than Squares.

BOTTOM LINE

Trends and systems are apples and oranges. Trends are much more Recency Bias-based, and don't have long term results. The systems discussed in this book have about 20 years of sample data from which to pull. Yes, Mr. Vaccaro, you know more about sports betting in your pinky finger than we ever will, but my personal history says we CAN use SYSTEMS (not trends) in sports betting to make a profit.

SIDE HUSTLE

WHAT TO PLAY

There are 4 major sports that I play throughout the calendar year: The National Football League, college football, Major League Baseball, and college basketball. The other sports, I play sporadically. The first thing you may notice is there is no mention of the National Basketball Association. I will bet the NBA Playoffs, because I know each team will play all their players and give a full effort. That doesn't apply to the regular season, especially now. I used to handicap regular season NBA in the past, but it has become WAY too difficult. Gone are the days when players started all 82 regular season games. In fact, in the 2022-23 NBA regular season, only 10 players played in 82 regular season games. 20 years prior, 46 players played in all 82 regular season games. Load Management has become a thing, and it makes for a more difficult game to handicap. To handicap NBA games, you truly must hustle this Side Hustle. In other words, a handicapper must keep up with what teams are doing. These days, point spreads can change several points from mornings of games to just before gametime. This is based on late injury news, and certain players just simply not playing for whatever reason. As stated earlier, if I had 10 hours a day to do this, I could. But like you, I don't. That's why I now wait until the playoffs to play NBA games, because it takes way too much time and effort to keep up with the playing statuses for each team.

INFORMATION BASED WAGERS: NFL Draft and NBA Draft

In 1990, I had just moved to Atlanta. As I started attending church, there was a program at my church where college kids who were from other places were assigned a "mentor" to confide in while progressing through school. After talking to me, they set me up with a huge sports fan. Go figure! But he was a huge boxing fan, and even went to the desert to see the big fights. He would take his wife, who would tolerate his love of boxing to get free spa days at the biggest hotels in the desert. They were wonderful people that I remained in contact with until the days they passed away in the 2010's. Again, life is about relationships.

Earlier in 1990, James "Buster" Douglas had knocked out Mike Tyson in the infamous fight in Tokyo where Jimmy Vaccaro had made Douglas a 42-1 underdog to Tyson. ESPN even did a 30 for 30 documentary on that fight, which anyone who was alive at the time remembers very well as one of the biggest upsets in the history of sports, not just boxing. Buster Douglas, a relative unknown to the world outside of boxing, was the heavyweight champion of the world!

Flash forward a few months. My mentor and his wife were heading to the desert to see Douglas and Atlanta's own Evander Holyfield face off for the title. Just before they left, I was told to sit by the phone in case they got any information that could help me make a couple of dollars on the fight. I dismissed it as crazy talk. What information? It's a fight, and Buster Douglas wasn't going to lose! Douglas had just defeated the unbeatable Mike Tyson a few months earlier!

But something had happened to Buster Douglas between the Tyson fight and the weigh-in to the Holyfield fight. All summer long, Douglas was on all the talk shows, and apparently was eating a lot of pizza. At the weigh-in a couple of days before the fight, Buster Douglas weighed almost 20 pounds more than he did for the Mike Tyson fight. 20 pounds? 20 pounds of all muscle, right? No, 20 pounds of marinara sauce from all those pizzas. Word has it that he was ordering pizzas to the ring while he was sparring in preparations for the fight. While Holyfield weighed in looking like a bodybuilder cut from granite. Douglas was the favorite before that fight, but after the weigh-in people were stampeding to the sports books to get their action down on Holyfield.

My mentor called me immediately after the weigh-in and asked me if I could get any action down, and I said I could. He made me promise to get something down on Holyfield before the guys in Atlanta got word that the line was moving due to Buster Douglas being fat. I said OK. At the time, I had a very small amount of money to my name at the time. I had double that amount bet on the Holyfield-Douglas fight. Now that's pressure! By the time the fight started, Holyfield had become the favorite over Douglas, a rarity in boxing that a champion would be an underdog to someone who had never been champion. When Holyfield walked out to the ring that night to an MC Hammer song, I knew everything was going to be fine.

Holyfield knocked out Douglas in 3 rounds, with Douglas apparently quitting when he could have gotten up. Holyfield was the champ, Douglas would never fight for a title again, and my mentor was a genius because he had the information before others did by attending the weigh-in. Information meant more before the internet than it does now because everyone gets the information in an instant these days. But following the money is important with wagers we can profit from, like the NFL and NBA Drafts.

The NFL and NBA Drafts are becoming betting events of their own now as well. The 2002 NBA Draft was Exhibit A for being able to discern information.

On the day of the draft, Paolo Banchero was favored to go number 1 overall to the Orlando Magic, but ESPN NBA Insider

SIDE HUSTLE

Adrian Wojnarowski did something that tore up the betting world. Woj tweeted early on the morning of the draft that it was "increasingly firm" that Jabari Smith would go first, Chet Holmgren would go second and Banchero would go third, before reversing course on his reporting 30 minutes before the draft began.

The chaos was palpable in the sports betting world. Woj never makes mistakes! This must be how it's going to go! We've got to get on this ASAP!

Sports books took several markets down, including the odds to go No. 1 overall. When some re-opened with Smith as high as −10000 to go first, with Banchero at +900. But the Sharps were not convinced by this Woj Bomb. In fact, the odds on Banchero kept plummeting throughout the day though no one other than Woj had this information.

Woj was silent until he tweeted again at 7:40 p.m. ET that Banchero had joined Smith Jr. under "serious consideration" to go No. 1 overall, which began moving the betting markets again, with more money flowing in on Banchero. Shortly thereafter, Banchero emerged again as the odds-on favorite to go No. 1.

At 7:42, Woj tweeted that Banchero had "emerged as a significant possibility to be drafted No. 1 overall."

At 7:55, five minutes before the draft was set to begin, Woj tweeted that Banchero was "looming as a frontrunner to be the No. 1 overall pick."

At 8:00 ET, Banchero was indeed taken No. 1 overall by the Magic. He closed as the favorite to go first, after Smith was −10000 earlier in the day.

A chaotic day that proved that the Sharps are always in the know. The Squares took in the Woj Bomb and their bankrolls were blown up for it. The Sharps stayed with Banchero, and even got him at a better

SIDE HUSTLE

price after the Woj Bomb. For NFL or NBA Drafts, following the LATE money is always the way to go. The information is out there. Someone is going to profit from it. Just watch, pay attention, and be able to discern credible information!

SIDE HUSTLE

MAKING THE BETS

Walking into a sports book can be an intimidating process, especially if you've never been to one before. The best warning that I can give new sports bettors going to a sports book for the first time is to make sure you have a game plan when you walk in. The boards will be filled with games and betting options. It can take you out of your game very quickly. Upon walking into the book, make sure you know what you are going to bet on before you arrive. That helps tremendously, especially for new bettors.

Find the rotation number: grab a sheet or look on the board for the game.

Walk to the window say number, and amount you want to bet. The sheets are old. Check the boards as you walk up to the window.

426 UCLA   +6   +180
427 USC   -6   58   -210

As you can see, USC is the home team (teams listed 2nd or at the bottom is the home team. By the way, that works when watching a game on television as well. The team listed on the score on the bottom or 2nd is the home team). USC is favored by 6 over UCLA, the point total for the game is 58. The money line price is $210 to win $100 if you want to bet on USC, and a $100 bet on UCLA winning the game straight up wins $180. Of course, you're not required to bet $100 on the money line. It's just how they are listed.

If you wanted to play the road underdog UCLA getting the 6 points, you would simply go to the window and say: "426 UCLA point spread $110 to win $100." It doesn't have to be that exact. You could also say "$110 426 spread." Anyone can do this if you can communicate the basics: team rotation number, amount of money to be risked, type of bet.

But going to the sports books are no longer just talking to someone behind the window. Kiosks, or things that look like old school arcade games are everywhere in sports books now that keep people from having to stand in long lines and allow bettors to place their bets by pressing buttons. This is a major advantage for bettors looking to get their action down quicker, but you must be able to maneuver through a computer screen. I have always said that as I grow older, it's very important to stay on top of modern technology as much as possible.

Make sure to check your ticket before you leave the window. Did you get the right amount? Did you get the betting line you thought you were going to get?

SIDE HUSTLE

HOW WE PLAY THE GAMES

THE NFL

(Editor's Note: When going over systems, the ones that I play blindly every time have the *Asterisk in front of them)

"The NFL: The league where they play.......for pay." - Mike Francesa

Of course, a sports talk radio host could not go through an entire book about sports gambling and not make at least one reference to Mike Francesa. These days, it's easy to mock him: from retiring more times than Sugar Ray Leonard only to return, to falling asleep on guests, the Diet Coke obsession, his love/hate relationship with Chris "Mad Dog" Russo, his love of Jason Giambi, his failed pay app (true fans will insert an $8.99 joke here), and the list goes on and on. But Francesa was one of the pioneers of sports talk radio who parlayed it into a bigger gig, appearing on CBS Television late 80's-early 90's on their college football and college basketball coverage. ESPN even did a *30 for 30* documentary on them, cementing them as sports talk radio legends. They will always be seen as the biggest local sports talkers in the history of the genre.

SIDE HUSTLE

But where Francesa was truly able to shine was when he went solo on his *The NFL Now* show on Sunday mornings before NFL kickoff. And right before he would go into the part where he would make his picks for the day, he would say the quote given above to make it sound much more important than it really was. And then, here comes the dramatic NFL Films music that always made any football fan stand at attention. It was as if we, as sports gamblers, were about to take the field just like the players. Except our battlefield was trying to get that money. But that was a different time, and a different place, whether we like it or not.

Now, everybody plays for pay. And everybody bets sports, but more people bet the NFL than anything. Wise Guys have been handing out parlay cards to sharps for decades. There is no bigger sport to handicap than the National Football League. People will argue "soccer" is the biggest sport in the world, and they have a valid argument. Just look at the action the desert gets when the World Cup is played every 4 years. But over a third of all money invested in sports in the state of Nevada comes from the NFL. And it's the easiest sport to bet as well. It always has been, and for the foreseeable future, it will continue to be so.

But the NFL is a very tough sport to take advantage of every single year and make a profit. It's the only sport where it might make some sense to possibly take a team because they are "due" to win. Usually, that's a terrible reason to bet on a certain team, but this is the NFL where very little makes sense on a week-to-week basis.

The NFL isn't my favorite sport to handicap, because I do better at a few other sports. In fact, some of the best handicappers in the world won't even touch the NFL. And there's nothing wrong with that whatsoever. Like we said earlier, do what's best for your bankroll. You don't have to bet the biggest gambling league in the world. The money you make on a Big Sky Conference basketball game played on a Tuesday night in February can be just as profitable as the Super Bowl!

These are the systems I use every year in the NFL, and have proven to grind out a profit over time:

THE BASICS

Home ain't where the heart is: Home teams cover more than road teams in the NFL, right? Have you not been paying attention? Road teams in the NFL cover 51.5% of the time since 2003 in a sample size of over 5,000 games.

Barking Dogs: In this same sample of over 5,000 games, underdogs have covered the spread 51.1% of the time. As we focus on all the point spread sports, home teams are overvalued, and favorites are overvalued. Get used to thinking that way, no matter what the media or conventional thinkers try to tell you. The data says otherwise.

Fading The Public: Simply going against the masses doesn't always win in the NFL. In a sample size of over 5,000, the team receiving the minority of bets (less than 50%) is only cashing tickets 50.2% of the time (2449-2431-133). The further away from 50% that number is, the better the chances at covering the spread it. But it isn't the end all, be all. It helps in the postseason, which we will address later. This goes against what most contrarians think because the NFL is the most public sport to bet, and the public is wrong more than right. But REALLY fading the public can be profitable. Taking underdogs getting less than 25% of the public money has hit 53.8% since 2003. It isn't a straight blind play every time for me, but it's something I consider when handicapping.

SIDE HUSTLE

THE SYSTEMS

Division Road Dogs: And if we take this theory to a higher level, we can turn a consistent profit. Divisional games turn these advantages of being on the road and being an underdog into a profitable system. In division games, road underdogs cover at a high level since 2003:

*Division road underdogs   634-544-35, 53.8%

Some may look at this and see 53.8% and say this isn't a huge advantage. But with a sample size of over 1,200 games, grinding out this profit on an annual basis makes for a successful system in the long term. And the public will be against us most of the time, which is exactly what we want.

In the NFL, we have key numbers. And those numbers are "3" and "7." Wagering NFL games is a completely different animal than betting on college football. About a quarter of NFL games end with a winning margin of exactly 3 or 7 points. However, that doesn't mean you should blindly bet any 7.5-point or more underdog. NFL underdogs getting exactly 3.5 points since 2003 cover 50.5% of the time. And underdogs getting exactly 7.5 points cover 49.5% of the time. Both of those trends will lose money. Having said that, squares will jump on dogs every time they see a 3.5 or a 7.5-point line. That can make money, but we must filter the data further to find a consistent profit.

So why were we talking about these Magic Numbers of 3 and 7. For those of you who play teasers, and that's more of you than should be playing them, I refer you to the great Stanford Wong. Wong wrote a book called Sharp Sports Betting many years ago. In that book, he detailed his 6-point NFL teasers based on the key numbers of 3 and 7. Basically, when you see an underdog of 1.5, 2 or 2.5 points, tease that team up through the 3 and 7 to get them at 7.5, 8, or 8.5. And when you see a favorite of 7.5, 8, or 8.5, tease them down through the 3 and 7 to get them as 1.5, 2, or 2.5-point favorites. A simple concept that was very profitable for a long time. But the books got wind of this and changed the game on us. When Wong wrote about his teasers, a bettor could get them at +100 or –110 juice. Now, a –120 juice on a 2-team teaser is the best line available. In other words, the books had to limit their losses on such a solid bet. Now, you have to win close to 55% to make a profit, instead of 50% at +100. If you haven't been paying attention, this makes a HUGE difference. So, while the Wong teaser is still a solid play, the desert has made it much more difficult to make a profit off these 6-point teasers. Buyer beware!

Short Road Dogs: Here's an example of how Home Field Advantage is often a good thing for us contrarians. The conventional wisdom of "Oddsmakers give 3 points to the Home Team" is flawed logic. The best home teams have bigger home field advantages than the worst home teams. But anytime we see a road dog between 2.5 and 3.5 points, we are ready to pounce. Since 2003, short road dogs cash tickets:

*Road Dogs between 2.5 and 3.5 points   483-404-49, 54.5%

In a sample size of over 900 games, this is a nice moneymaker that can take the guess work out of which team should be favored in a matchup of teams that have similar power ratings in the desert.

The Sharp Money: Look for an underdog getting at least 10% more money than tickets. Following this since 2003 has hit 54.5% of the time ATS. Again, it's not a blind automatic play every time, but it helps in handicapping.

Reverse Line Move: When a line moves 1.5 points towards that team (example: going from +3 to +1.5, or from –2 to –3.5), and that team has received less than 40% of the public money, those teams cover the spread 54.6% of the time since 2005.

Overreaction Theatre: Give us your tired, your poor, and your hungry. In other words, the current media landscape loves teams that won last week. But more importantly, they hate teams that lost last week. And the worse that team lost, the more panic that runs through the streets. But these are exactly the teams we love to play the following week.

Since 2003, when a team loses the previous week by 12 points or more, they cash tickets the next week:

*Road dogs after 12+ point loss   377-302-19, 55.5%

Buy low, sell high. The team that lost big last week can make us money this week. Once you can wrap your arms around this concept, especially in the NFL, you'll do very well.

Overreaction Theatre 2, The Wrath of The Desert: I can still see Ricardo Montalban and William Shatner yelling at each other in *Star Trek II: The Wrath of Khan*. But to me, Montalban was always the guy who somehow got Reggie Jackson to try to kill the Queen of England back in the day. And for my money, the baseball scene in *The Naked Gun* might be the best sports 15 minutes in movie history, but that's another story for Enrico Pallazzo another day. Since 2003, if a road dog lost ATS by 6 points or more the previous week, they're a good bet to cash a ticket the next week:

*Road Dogs that lost ATS by 6 or more previous week
604-518-29, 53.8%

The media is against these teams, and the gamblers are upset with them because they lost ATS by a ton. Those scorned gamblers probably gave up on this team the previous week by halftime and won't bet on them the next week for anything. A perfect time to take one man's trash and make it our treasure.

A Fortnight of Rest: I will admit it. I learned what "fortnight" meant when I was a kid because the late Dick Enberg would describe Wimbledon as a "fortnight" and it lasted 14 days. I figured it out on my own. Sometimes, that's how we learn to succeed at sports gambling as well: we must learn things on our own the hard way.

But as much as we like to take the road dogs in the NFL, the bye weeks throw a wrench into that system. When a team has 14 or more days off during the regular season, they come out on fire after the long rest. But the profitable play is when that team off the bye week is the favorite. Did you say favorite? Yes, the numbers don't lie! Taking favorites off a 14-day rest hits 56.4% of the time (171-132-8). Filtering it down further, road favorites off a full 14-day or more rest since 2003 are 69-38-2 ATS (64.5%). Road dogs are great, but we can't just blindly take them all and expect to make a profit. We must look for our spots.

Regression To the Mean: If a team has been lousy straight up all season, the squares line up to bet against them. This is a big mistake.

*Road Dogs with Straight Up Win % of 40% or less
764-665-31, 53.5%

The media influences the squares, and the media loves piling on dumpster fires. But those dumpster fires often cash tickets.

SIDE HUSTLE

Regression To The Mean 2: Spread Loser's Boogaloo: In the same ilk, look at a team's record ATS. When a team has covered the spread 44% of the time or less for the season, they are prime to cash a ticket.

*Road Dogs with ATS Win % of 44% or less
747-635-36, 54.1%

If a team burns a bettor's ticket in September, it might keep that same bettor from betting on them in November. That's the way losers think. The goal of the oddsmakers is to have every NFL team hit 50% ATS, much like Pete Rozelle wanted every NFL team to win 50% of their games back in the day. Parity exists in the real NFL, and in the desert. Every dog has his day.

On The Road Again: Long trips on the road are taxing on anyone, much less some of the best athletes in the world. So it's obvious that a team on the 2nd game of a 2 week road game streak in consecutive weeks will struggle much more in the 2nd game than the 1st, right? Wrong again! That conventional wisdom fails us again! Since 2003, road underdogs on the 2nd leg of a 2-game road trip cash the tickets:

*Road Dogs on road for 2nd consecutive week
476-411-22, 53.7%

Once again, a big sample size of over 800 games, all debunking what we think should be the case. These are exactly the kind of systems that can turn a losing bettor into a winning one, because they go against what we are raised to believe by the media.

SIDE HUSTLE

You down with YPP?: Yeah, you know me! Naughty By Nature had their 15 minutes back in the early 90's, but they had no idea what YPP was. YPP is Yards Per Play, and the best football handicappers use this number quite a bit to determine how good a team really is. The key number here is 5. Since 2003, look for road dogs that average more than 5 yards per play.

*Road Dogs avg 5+ yds per play
777-667-31, 53.8%

Defense wins championships, right? We are taught that from Day 1. But the numbers tell us that Road Dogs that can move the ball cash more tickets. When you hear the term "Backdoor Cover," it was made for road dogs that score just enough to cover the spread.

Stanley Roper breaking the 4th wall: One of the first TV shows I remember was Three's Company. There's a lot of politcal incorrectness in that show, but it's too late now. But the best part of that show is when the landlord of the apartments, Mr. Roper, would insult his wife and look into the camera and smile. It was stupid, silly, and I loved it. Speaking of Reinventing Yourself, Suzanne Somers leaving Three's Company back in the day was one of the worst career moves ever, right up there with Shelley Long leaving Cheers, but I digress.

Anyway, "Breaking The 4th Wall" is when an actor acknowledges the existence of the audience and speak to them directly. Zack Morris did this often when he called time outs on Saved By The Bell, but Mr. Roper was the best. And I think of him every time we play this next system.

It's simple. Any team that has lost exactly 3 games in a row, take them ATS in the 4th game. Since 2003, it's made us money.

SIDE HUSTLE

*Dogs on 3-game straight up losing streaks
204-146-10, 58.3%

The theory is that the public has lost all faith in the team on the 3-game losing streak and refuses to bet on that team to cover in Game 4. This gives the dog extra value. And don't even think about telling me Mr. Furley was better than Mr. Roper, because them's fightin' words!

TOTALS

Squares often dismiss totals, and don't play them. This is a mistake, as there are profitable systems to employ with the number of points scored in these NFL games. Overall, since 2003, going the "under" the total has hit 50.6% of the time. That doesn't make anyone a profit.

You also don't want to have the mindset that NFL rules changes have made it so easy for quarterbacks that you can't even bet Unders. The market knows about the rules changes. Besides, it's possible to help a quarterback in a way that generates Unders if it's helping him run clock with short passes that move the chains in the fourth quarter.

And stop thinking that the NFL protects their quarterbacks (and they do) to make it easy for them to score big points, so nobody should ever bet the under. The market has already accounted for this. That goes for any conventional wisdom: the oddsmakers have already reacted to any brilliant idea we come up with on the spot.

Totals can be very tricky for casual bettors, who tend to bet with the eye test instead of using data. Then they treat totals like coin flips. If they see a team is playing well, they will take them to go over the total. Others think under is ready to hit, and bet that way based on that line of reasoning.

How should a good handicapper approach betting totals? Game conditions and the betting market.

You can do a ton of work determining that the total should be a certain number, only to find out the betting market is way ahead of you. We can't outthink the Sharps, but we can make it so that we profit from them.

Division Unders: Going under in divisional games since 2003 proves profitable over the years, given the total is 41 or more:

*Under 41 or more in division games
754-638-23 54.2%

With a sample size of over 1,400, grinding out this 54.2% system makes a bettor money. The concept is that familiarity breeds contempt, hence the games are played tighter. The numbers agree.

And look out for weather! Conventional wisdom says that when the weather turns cold in the northern, non-dome stadiums, that the point totals collapse. This is true, but the cold temperatures aren't the factor. The wind means everything.

Only recently has the market started paying more attention to this. Any stadium with swirling or gusty winds will wreak havoc on the passing game and field goal attempts.

And the moment rain or snow is included in the game day forecast, you'll see the total for that game drop 2-3 points almost immediately. Only recently has the market started paying more attention to wind, and the numbers speak for themselves.

Cutting Wind: Since 2003, going "under" the total in any game with a 10 MPH wind or higher means the offenses have problems:

*Under in games with 10+ MPH winds
604-484-8, 55.5%

Here's another system where you don't need to know the first thing about anything other than watching The Weather Channel. Do people do that anymore? How about accessing your weather app on your phone? That works. Our apologies to Jim Cantore.

The Sharp Money: Following the markets allows the Sharps to lead us to the money for NFL totals. When the amount of money on the under in the desert is 10% more than the number of tickets on the under since 2016:

*Under when Money 10%+ more than Tickets
278-194-5, 58.9%

Betting totals isn't like flipping coins. Following the markets and the weather can lead to cashing a lot of tickets during the NFL season.

THE BOTTOM LINE

The NFL can be fickle, but looking to go with road teams, underdogs, and under totals (all especially in divisional matchups) can limit losses long term and help you get to a profitable position in the NFL. Recency Bias looms larger in the NFL than any other sport as well. The quicker a sports gambler can forget what happened last week, the more likely that bettor is to win next week.

COLLEGE FOOTBALL

"You can have all the scat backs you want, but give me the Big Uglies down in the trenches!" - The Late College Football Announcer Keith Jackson

SIDE HUSTLE

Everybody had a Keith Jackson impression back in the day. It seemed like he did all the big college football games when I was growing up. He wasn't from the south, but he always felt like he was when he would do those SEC games. And Keith Jackson knew teams needed to be tough up front. But just like in the NFL, they need a good quarterback too.

I refer to this quite often on my radio show. In 2014, Todd Gurley of Georgia was the favorite to win the Heisman Trophy at midseason. He was doing it all, from running, receiving, to even running back kickoffs. And Georgia was rolling too, being ranked in the Top 10. At midseason, Georgia was traveling to Missouri. The line in the desert was Georgia –3. Missouri was coming off 2 straight trips to the SEC Championship Game, so this game was very important. After the line came out with Georgia –3, Gurley got busted for signing autographs. It seems silly in today's NIL world, doesn't it? The desert immediately took the game off the board while waiting on word if Gurley would play. On Friday of that week, 24 hours before the game, Gurley was declared ineligible by the NCAA. And the desert put the game back up on the board, with Georgia STILL a 3-point favorite over Missouri. Think about it! Here is the FAVORITE for the HEISMAN TROPHY declared out. And the line does not change a single half point. THAT should tell you that college football is about scheduling, recruiting, coaching, and quarterbacking. Exhibit A, your honor. Georgia won the game 34-0, but the point was crystal clear: don't bother the desert with your drama unless your quarterback is out.

Here's Exhibit B. Keep in mind that injuries are not required to be reported like it is in the NFL. But also keep in mind that The Desert knows more than the local media does. Here in Lexington in 2022, Kentucky was preparing to play South Carolina. On Monday, the line was Kentucky −10.5. But when whispers about Kentucky's quarterback Will Levis potentially missing the game surfaced, this line dropped like a rock. And before it hit the local media, the lines had already been adjusted in the desert. Kentucky's coach Mark Stoops was asked about Levis' injury on Thursday of that week, and Stoops started yelling at the reporter who asked the question wondering aloud if the reporter wanted him to give away his game plan as well. Stoops said he would tell us if Levis wasn't going to play. Levis never played but Stoops never told us either. At kickoff, Kentucky was only a 4.5-point favorite, a touchdown difference from where the line opened. And Levis wasn't in the running for any Heisman Trophy either. That just signifies how important the quarterbacks in college football are. Kentucky lost to South Carolina 24-14, but another point was made: college football coaches don't have to tell the media anything about injuries. So don't expect them to say anything. And if they do, it probably won't be anything truthful. But in most cases, The Desert will tell you if a quarterback is playing or not. All you need to do is pay attention.

As big of a sport as the NFL is in this country, there are places (especially in the South) where College Football is the biggest sport. But using the same systems in the pros and the colleges is comparing apples to oranges. We now live in the time of Transfer Portals and NIL. Schools can go out and buy players and fleece other teams for top talent. It's truly the Wild Wild West! One of the best preseason college football publications that handicappers have used for years has been Phil Steele's Preseason Magazine. It's incredible the work that must go into putting that together. But now, with all the turmoil and player movement, even that publication must take even more hustle than just 5 years ago.

SIDE HUSTLE

College football might be the 2nd most popular sport to wager, but I prefer wagering the college game as opposed to the NFL.

As much as the NFL rules the American Sports Betting landscape, college football is the 2nd most popular sport on which to wager in this country. In other words, football rules.

Having said that, comparing handicapping college football to the NFL is flawed logic. It's apples and oranges. Parity rules in the NFL. Teams that are bad one year, can dominate the next. But in college football, the same teams are at the top every single year. Teams like Alabama, Georgia, and Ohio State have been consistently good for several years, no matter who the players are. How is that? Recruiting. College sports is about recruiting and coaching, before all else. With the new Transfer Portal rules in college football, and the college football playoff expanding to 12 teams, maybe we see a more balanced landscape in the future. But for now, the giants remain the giants.

College football is inherently apples and oranges when compared to the NFL. In the NFL, new teams rise from the ashes every season. In college football, it's the same old song and dance every year. Alabama, Ohio State, Clemson, and Oklahoma have qualified for the college football playoff a combined 21 times. Every other team in the nation combined have qualified 11 times. Yet, college football always proclaims that "Every Game Matters" and they have the most important and relevant regular season.

The NFL has 32 teams. College football has well over 100 FBS teams. With over 60 teams in the Power 5 Conferences.

And unlike the NFL, the revolving door at quarterback often gives teams flawed power rating values, especially early in the season.

The Phil Steele Preseason Magazine has been a staple for football handicappers for many years now. It truly was the one publication that a college football handicapper could trust throughout the season. But in the current age of transfer portals and mass player movement, this must be one of the most difficult publications to keep accurate.

One of the traps we fall into in the summertime is putting too much value in win totals for the coming season. And why do we do that? Because a sports gambler has a tough time during July and August. Sure, Major-League Baseball is entering the Dog Days of Summer, but they've been playing every day for months now. And during July and August, sports gamblers have the attention span of a hungry dog surrounded by treats. All we do is grind our picks out in MLB, then turn our attention to the upcoming NFL and college football seasons.

Coach

Quarterback

Schedule (who they play, where they play them, when they play them)

Recruiting rankings

As a sports talk radio host, I detest discussing recruiting rankings on the air. Why does anyone need to know about some.

Having said that, recruiting is the lifeblood of any college football program. If you don't have the Jimmy's and Joe's, it doesn't matter about the X's and O's.

THE BASICS

In the NFL, we see a distinct advantage in road underdogs long term. In college football, that is not the case. Since 2005, underdogs have covered the spread 50.3% of the time in a sample size of over 13,000 games (6,727-6,644-225).

In those same years since 2005, college football road teams cover the spread 51% of the time (6,661-6,402-217).

SIDE HUSTLE

The Public handles their money better in college football, with our Fade The Public minority of bets (less than 50% of the money) hitting 50.2% of the time. While road dogs and fading the public win more than they lose in both the NFL and college football, neither are blind moneymakers. And the NFL gets you closer to the magical 52.38% line than the colleges offer.

The Sharp Money: When looking for disparities in tickets purchased vs money wagered, we always look for the more money wagered as being the sharp money. With the money wagered is 10% or more than the ticket numbers in college football, the sharp money wagered cashes 52% of the tickets since 2016 (1,362-1,257-32).

THE SYSTEMS

Home Field Advantage?: Since 2005, in a sample size of over 13,000 games, road teams in college football cover the spread 50.9% of the time. That's a far cry from 52.38%. Once again, road teams in college football have more value in the desert than home teams. Stop us if you've heard this before.

David edges Goliath in a Split Decision: In a sample of over 14,000 games since 2005, underdogs have covered the spread 50.3% of the time. So, while it isn't the sizeable advantage like it is in the NFL, college football road teams and underdogs still offer a slight value.

I'm a Man! I'm well into my 50's now!: Which coach in college football cashes the most tickets? Easy question, right? It must be Nick Saban. Saban has made us money, but he's not the best. If not him, Dabo Swinney? Swinney: also good, but not the biggest moneymaker. Which college coach is the best moneymaker in the desert? Mike Gundy of Oklahoma State! You remember him! HE yelled "I'm a man! I'm 40!" That was a long time ago, as his mullet will attest. Here is Gundy's record ATS:

SIDE HUSTLE

*Mike Gundy ATS Oklahoma State   129-96-0, 57.3%

It should send a strong message that Gundy's record is 57.3% ATS and he is the best coach in the nation at making money. It also sends a message that Gundy cashes tickets while never making a College Football Playoff or winning a conference championship. The money is out there, we just have to find it. I don't play Gundy and Oklahoma State every game, but I take this into consideration before playing on or against them, especially when Oklahoma State is a favorite.

With that said, College Football doesn't have full parity yet. There's always the Cupcake Games early in the season when the Power 5 Goliath's trying to pound the lowly non-Power 5 David's into submission. While we love taking those big underdogs in the NFL, the Cupcakes in College Football don't have the same appear or cash the same number of tickets

Having said that, we do look to take some favorites and home teams in college football. While the numbers favor underdogs and road teams in the NFL, there is very little difference with these in the colleges. The line is always the great equalizer, and as always the oddsmakers are on top of things.

College Football, like any college sport, is about recruiting. Nick Saban couldn't win national championships with Vanderbilt's roster. But Saban would go out and recruit a national championship roster immediately. And with the current state of rosters, it's tough to handicap teams with so much turnover from year to year. But recruiting rankings can help determine the value of a roster. As a sports talk radio host in an SEC town, people LOVE to talk about recruiting 15–18-year-old kids. This drives me crazy. A lot of these kids who commit to schools won't show up on campus for over 2 years, but the fanbase is giddy just thinking about them showing up. Keep in mind, we went through COVID-19 in less time than between some of these kids announcing their college plans and showing up to play. How many tickets am I going to cash between now and then? I'm worried about today, not tomorrow. Sometimes, we lose perspective and can't see the forest for the trees. OK, I'm off the college fanbase soap box for now!

Short Road Dogs: Remember, we are playing numbers not teams! In college football since 2005, underdogs of 5.5 points or less have done very well ATS:

*Road Dogs between 1 and 5.5 points ATS
1027-897-29, 53.4%

The sample size of over 1,900 games proves this is a long-term moneymaker. Anything 5.5 points or less is the "sweet spot" for this system.

Pollsterized: Ah yes, the wonderful Top 25 AP Poll. I know someone who votes in the AP Top 25 College Football Poll. In fact, I do a radio segment every blue moon trying to figure out why he voted for certain teams where he did. But this is a difficult duty, because it's a Subjective task, not an Objective one. The best sports gamblers play against the AP Poll, both college football and basketball, at every opportunity. But in college football, the real value lies in playing the favorites in games between ranked teams since 2005:

*Favorites in matchups between AP Top 25 teams
435-359-15, 54.8%

See, we can take favorites (sometimes). With a sample size of over 800 games, the desert tells us who the better team is no matter who is ranked higher.

Every Number Tells A Story, Don't It?: Rod Stewart never got enough credit. Look at that guy, and please tell me how he dated so many hot ladies back in the day! If this guy was digging ditches, he wouldn't be able to get a date from a calendar, but I digress from jealousy! Road dogs are our favorites, but there are live dogs and dead dogs. The trick is to find the live dogs and avoid the dead ones. A proven way to find those diamonds in the rough is to look at the totals to these games. Games with low totals allow for very little wiggle room for home favorites to play with, and the magic number is 53.5 for our purposes. Since 2005, road underdogs in college football do well when the total for the game is 53.5 or less:

*Road Dogs with a total of 53.5 or less
2082-1872-58, 52.7%

With a sample size of almost 4,000 games, only hitting 52.7% is enough to make a nice profit. Also keep in mind, that the lower the total is under 53.5, the better those percentages of wins become. In other words, the lower the total, the better chance the road dog has to cover the spread.

Bye Bye Bye: Although I'm an expert on 80's and 90's music, I had checked out by the Boy Band Era. The worst traffic jam I was ever in was on a Saturday night in Atlanta when the Braves had a home game, the Hawks had a home playoff game, and one of these Boy Bands filled up the Georgia Dome. Like Ron Burgundy drinking milk in the San Diego sun, that was a bad choice.

SIDE HUSTLE

Just like the NFL, we look to play teams coming off a bye week. But unlike the NFL, we are looking to play home favorites. Schools with 14-15 days off since their previous game, and then are favored at home, those are the teams that cash the tickets since 2005:

*Home Favorites with 14-15 days off between games
374-313-15, 54.4%

The difference between 18–22-year-old college kids having 2 weeks off then playing a home game in front of their friends and family is a different story than professionals getting time off to rest than going on a business trip. One of many reasons why handicapping the colleges is different than the pros.

YPP Hop Hooray!: Another Naughty By Nature reference, for those of you who aren't down when I thought I was cool back in the day. My apologies in advance. But in college football, look for Yards Per Play stats to find winners. And like in the NFL, the magic number for this stat is 5. Road underdogs that average 5 yards per play or more, facing teams that don't average 5 yards per play, do very well ATS since 2005:

*Road Dogs that avg 5+ yds per play at teams that avg <5 yds per play
775-673-17, 53.5%

We are getting the better team statistically that the betting public doesn't think will win. And with a sample size of over 1,400, it's a proven winner.

Road Dogs on the moneyline

Team A is favored over Team B by 4 points or less. Team A is at home.

Conventional Thinking: Team A is the home team. Team A is favored. More than likely, the majority of the public is on Team A. It's a "safe" pick

Contrarian Thinking: Team B is the choice on the moneyline. If they win the game, I'll get more bang for my buck.

History says: If you do NOTHING but take Road Underdogs of 4 points of less on the moneyline since 2005, you'd "only" win 47% of the time (711-803). But your ROI for these games is 6% in a sample size of over 1500 games.

They're Heating Up! They're On Fire! Fans of the NBA Jam video game from back in the day can hear that voice yelling those phrases now. NBA Jam is on the level just below RBI Baseball and Tecmo Bowl as the best sports video games of all time, as previously discussed. But the announcer guy gives that game something the others don't.

Look out for the hot weather games in August and September. With the hot weather, scores go sky high as well. In games where the game time temperature is 90 degrees or more in August and September, the overs hit since 2005:

*Overs in August & September when the temp is 90 or more
122-89-2, 57.8%

As the weather cools down, so do the offenses. That's why we exploit this system while we can.

Drop And Give Me an Under!: The Service Academies play football the old-fashioned way, with running offenses and fast-moving clocks. Of course, when Army, Navy, and Air Force get together, it's double shot power of old timey football. This is a GREAT time to go under the totals. In fact, since 2005, the "under" has hit an incredible 81.1% (43-10-1) in matchups between any of the 3 Service Academies.

*Under the total in games between 2 of Army, Navy, and Air Force 43-10-1, 81.1%

    The media is all over this one now, unfortunately. You'll hear this a lot when these teams get together. It's like Yogi Berra said, "Nobody goes there anymore. It's too crowded." If you get that, you get why it may be time to be wary of this system.
    When these teams get together, the media will assuredly shove this stat down your throats about the "under" hitting so much in these games. But the desert has caught up with this system. The totals in the early years of these matchups were regularly in the 50's, with some reaching the 60's! But between 2020 and 2022, we saw 7 matchups between Army, Navy, and Air Force in the 30's. In other words, the oddsmakers have noticed this trend, and moved the line accordingly. So even though this is a GREAT system to play, keep an eye on the number the desert makes in these matchups. When the public wins 81.1% of the time in a matchup, the desert will make sure things change soon enough. Going under a total in the 50's is a lot easier than going under a total in the 30's. Make sure you aren't getting the worst of it when it comes to lines as more and more squares figure out this system.
    Winds Of Change: A song by The Scorpions, 1991, another song by a hard rocker band that cashed in on the "Every Bad Boy Has a Soft Side" mantra. You might remember that the lead singer whistles during the song. Why did these hard rockers stoop to such demeaning

levels? Because they made money hand over fist! Some might call them sellouts, but they are still cashing in off that song.

Well, the Winds Of Change can help us cash in as well! Just like in the NFL, we look for windy conditions. But in the college ranks, the magic number is 8. When a college game is played in 8 MPH winds or more, the unders cash the tickets

*Unders in games with 8+ MPH wins
2301-1981-52, 53.7%

That's a sample size of over 4,200 games. So while precipitation makes the squares run to the window, the sharps look more at the wind. Start looking at forecasts early in the week to get the better numbers on these totals.

"Aloha" means making money while you sleep: As we have established, I am a fan of no individual team. But I have always had a special place in my heart for Hawaii football. The 11-2 Hawaii team in 1992 taught me a lot of lessons about life, including a real player can make money while he/she sleeps. And since every Hawaii game started at 2AM Eastern Time back then, you had to be asleep for those! That Hawaii team also went 10-3 ATS, and I have no idea how a nice young man like me in school at the time would remember such numbers from decades ago, but I digress.

But those are the salad days for Hawaii football. Now, they don't cash tickets. And those desperate gamblers either looking to double down on their winnings from Saturday afternoon, or looking to get back what they lost, have taken it on the chin when investing in Hawaii football. Since 2005, Hawaii is 50-59-3 ATS at home. And they're 23-31-2 as a home favorite. Sound familiar? The warm weather also allows for high scoring, with the "over" hitting 55% (60-49-1) of the time in Hawaii home games. Although these aren't systems to blindly take to the bank after a big Saturday night out on the town, keep in mind history tells us Hawaii doesn't live up to expectations at home very often. And games on the islands tend to be high scoring. Aloha!

COLLEGE BASKETBALL

Meet your newest bestest buddy, Ken Pomeroy

On my radio show, we call Ken Pomeroy the "Lord and Savior of Basketball Analytics." We still love Jeff Sagarin, but KenPom (as he is known) has taken it to an entirely new level.

For serious basketball handicappers out there, I highly suggest paying the $20 fee to be able to access all his numbers. Look at the opening lines of every college basketball game in the desert and compare them the KenPom's FanMatch section where the scores are projected. The sides and totals are VERY similar to what KenPom projects. That's not a coincidence.

In fact, I've been following KenPom numbers for so long, that my log in is my old America Online email address. Insert Dial-Up Modem and "You've Got Mail" joke here.

Here are some basic records ATS for certain teams in college basketball:

Underdogs: 50%
Visitors: 50.5%
Underdogs and Visitors: 50.4%
Underdogs and Visitors in conference games: 51%

SIDE HUSTLE

What are you talking about? If you blindly do this, you'll never make money! True! That's why we have to filter them down further. The conference games, where schools are rivals and very familiar with each other, the numbers become more advantageous to the contrarian sports bettor.

It's as simple as that. Using 4 filters: conference games, visiting teams, underdogs, and the point spread is greater than what KenPom projects as the margin of victory for the game. If you do this, will you hit 60%? No. Again, unrealistic expectations. But you will get the best opportunity to make a profit during college basketball season. I've been using this for well over a decade, and it's worked very well for me.

College basketball is my favorite sport to handicap. Why? Because as much as the public doesn't believe this, it's the sport that follows the numbers as well as any of them. But we all remember the upsets in the NCAA Tournament. And we will get to handicapping NCAA Tournament games later.

Here is a system I've followed every year for a couple of decades now, and it's worked every single season for a profit except the COVID season of 2021.

Scenario: Team A vs Team B. The game and Team A fit the following criteria:

The game is a conference game.

Team A is the visiting team.

Team A is the underdog.

In January and February, almost every college basketball game has a game that fits these criteria. But as my old man used to warn me: "there are live dogs, and there are dead dogs."

SIDE HUSTLE

The bigger the conference, the better the results over time. The public is usually more wrong on the higher profile conference games than the smaller "cupcake" conferences.

Keep in mind that we are not the only ones who worship the ground of one Ken Pomeroy. A section on KenPom's site predicts the score of each day's games. You'll be amazed at how close the spreads and totals listed in the desert coincide with the projected scores from KenPom. That is total respect for the accuracy for KenPom's numbers.

But if we know about KenPom, the oddsmakers know all about him too. That's why we have to filter out times to use the KenPom numbers to our advantage. It's flawed logic to simply use KenPom to handicap every game that's off by a half point or more and just go from there.

The bigger the conference, the better the result. Because in the bigger leagues, the public tends to be more wrong. It's like how the public is always on the wrong side of the biggest sporting event on Earth, the Super Bowl.

College basketball is my favorite sport to handicap. Not because I grew up in Central Kentucky and the environment was college basketball crazy, but because I've had more success with this sport than the others. And whatever makes a bettor the most money, immediately becomes their favorite sport.

And this sport is a sport on the decline. When I was a kid in the 80's, every major network was filled with college basketball games all weekend long. ESPN made household names of players and coaches from the Big East Conference. Those of us that followed the sport knew the players on the big teams, because they stuck around for 4 years. Obviously, that has changed now with the Transfer Portal, NIL rules, and we simply don't live in the same world anymore.

SIDE HUSTLE

Or do we? In 2023, there were exactly zero freshmen players starting on the 4 teams in the NCAA Final Four. And that isn't an outlier either! In 2019, only 1 freshman player started in the Final Four. So, while a lot of the infamous "blue blood" teams have

In college football, we refer to the Power 5 Conferences constantly. No school can win big long term if they aren't a Power 5 Team. In college basketball, we have a Power 6. The Big East Conference has earned their way into the pantheon of college basketball power conferences, on the strength of programs like Connecticut and Villanova this century.

In Division I college football, there are a little over 100 teams. In Division I college basketball, there are over 350 teams. On a normal Saturday in January and February, there are well over 100 college basketball games to choose from on the betting board. If a bettor "bets the entire board" on a Saturday, it's probably not in his/her best interest financially.

What do the Squares ask first when handicapping a game? Who is the home team? It isn't just college basketball, but Conventional Wisdom says the home teams have the bigger advantage in college basketball. Once again, the numbers prove people wrong.

Here is the ATS records for home teams and visiting teams during the college basketball regular season since the 2004-2005 season:

Visitor	28834-28296-1175	-2%
Home	28296-28834-1175	-3.9%

These numbers tell us that a bettor loses almost twice as much money betting on home teams in the regular season over the years than betting on road teams. With a sample size of over 58,000 games, we have enough historical data to make a conclusion.

This advantage becomes even more evident in conference games.

Here are the records ATS for home and visiting teams in **conference games only** since the 2004-2005 season:

Visitor	20741-20045-865	-1.3%
Home	20045-20741-865	-4.7%

Visiting teams have an advantage, and they have more of an advantage in conference games. That's exactly the opposite of Conventional Wisdom tells us.

That's OK, the Chalk Pushing Squares will rely on favorites to cash their tickets. Once again, Conventional Wisdom couldn't be more wrong.

Here are the ATS records of favorites and underdogs in regular season college basketball games since the 2004-2005 season:

Dog	32245-32315-1328	-3%
Favorite	32315-32245-1328	-3%

In over 65,000 games of sample size data, for the difference to be less than 100 games is quite amazing. But this includes all games whether they are conference and non-conference games.

Nothing in sports "gambling" is a guaranteed winner. But if you follow the following 4 filters, even someone who doesn't follow the game can potentially make a profit:

Conference games: Familiarity breed contempt.

Road Teams: The underdog mentality: look for the conference road dogs.

SIDE HUSTLE

KenPom: compare the conference road dogs to KenPom's projections.

Home court DISadvantage?: Once again, conventional wisdom loses when looking at ATS records for home teams in college basketball. Since 2005, road teams cover the spread 50.5% of the time (28834-28296-1175) in a sample size of over 58,000 regular games! That's a lot of data to sift through. And although the road teams don't blindly turn a profit, they cash tickets more often than home teams.

What do the Squares ask about first when they are asked to handicap a game? "Who's the home team?" And sure, this is a very important quality. However, the Squares put WAY too much value and emphasis on the home team in college basketball. And why not? Sleeping in your own bed, eating familiar meals, familiarity with the playing court and rims, and the home fans cheering them on loudly. It's a recipe for success. But if we know this, the desert knows it too. Squares LOVE taking the home teams, especially in college basketball. For that reason, more than any other, the Desert overvalues home teams. General knowledge and conventional wisdom say that home teams usually get 3-4 points added to their point spread value for having the home court advantage. Other teams get more than that. Teams with big home court advantages often get more than 3-4 points. And the best home court advantages (see Duke) often get anywhere between 6-8 points added to their perceived value, simply for playing at home. What does this add up to? Value for the road team.

Favorites? Really? YES!: In college basketball, the favorites cover more than the underdogs. But it's very close! Since 2005, favorites cover the spread 50.1% of the time (32315-32245-1328) in a crazy sample size of over 65,000 regular season games. In other words, there's no distinct advantage in underdogs or favorites in college basketball.

HOW WE PLAY COLLEGE BASKETBALL

More than anything in college basketball, coaching means everything. The best coaches in college basketball that you immediately think of aren't always the best ones to invest in long term.

Tony Bennett can send you from Rags To Riches (depending on the time of year): Virginia basketball under Tony Bennett is a riddle wrapped inside of an enigma. They are the 2019 NCAA Champions. Wrapped around that championship is a plethora of underachieving results in the NCAA Tournament, and a lot of burned brackets (mine included). But that is the Tournament, and it's a separate animal. In the regular season, Tony Bennett and Virginia is a big money-maker.

This is Bennett's record ATS in the regular season at UVA:

Tony Bennett ATS at Virginia in regular season
218-162-8, 57.4%

That great winning percentage improves when Virginia is playing games on the road, or when they are favored, or out of conference. It's the same recipe every year: good team playing tough defense, the public undervalues them in the desert, and UVA wins a lot of games and covers a lot of spreads. By the time March arrives, their resume is impeccable! Then they underachieve once the brackets come out. In other words, Bennett and Virginia is a great bet.....as long as the calendar doesn't say March.

Mmm, Cupcakes!: Ah yes, we love to eat the Cupcakes! On my radio show in Lexington, I refer to Rupp Arena as The Cupcake

Factory in November and December because The University of Kentucky basketball schedule is littered with several games each season where the home team powerhouse welcomes schools from far and wide that no one has ever heard of for a beat down that will give the home team yet another victory.

*Home Favorites Ranked AP 1-10 Non-Conference game in Nov. And Dec.
441-372-12, 54.2%

Here's a secret of the AP College Basketball Poll: always remember the very first preseason poll. There are times when the preseason poll is somehow better at predicting the NCAA Tournament than the final regular season poll. When the season starts, the best teams are ranked at the top before the conference season changes everything. That's one reason why we look to take advantage of the very best teams against the Cupcakes in the pre-conference schedule.

Fade The Top 3 in Conference!: In case you haven't noticed, we like division/conference matchups when looking to play the underdogs. In this system, we are looking to go against the very best teams in America. Anytime we see a team ranked 1-3 in the current AP Poll during the regular season, we look to fade them. But we only look to fade them in conference games since 2004.

*Conference Dogs facing teams ranked 1-3 in AP Poll
542-458-24, 54.2%

All the clichés fit here: it's the other team's Super Bowl facing the highly ranked powerhouse.

SIDE HUSTLE

Yo, Eleven!: At the craps table, most of the bettors like to hear the phrase "Yo, Eleven!" Unless you're one of those people who plays the "Don't Pass Line," which is always a point of debate for casino gamblers. Most people at the craps tables are playing with the shooter (the person rolling the dice) and playing the Pass Line. However, the slightly better percentage play is to bet the Don't Pass Line and rooting for the shooter to "crap out" by rolling a 7. The numbers tell us that's the better play, but you won't be very popular at the table. You're looking into someone eyes and saying, "I'm betting against you, loser!" A lot of people don't like that, understandably. Then again, it's dice! What do you expect? Craps players have all kinds of issues like that, and don't even think about just saying the word "seven" at the table or else you're jinxing everyone! Spoiler Alert: saying the word "seven" at the craps table doesn't change the way the dice land but try convincing 99% of the bettors that! They will curse you under their breath and stare at you as they leave the table broke, blaming you for all their problems in life! Of all the casino games, craps can be the most polarizing, but it is one of the few games in the casino that offer true odds. Those true odds bets are the bets you can place behind the pass line bets and come bets. Craps is a great casino game, but like MLB there's a lot of unwritten rules! My theory for craps starts like sports gambling, then differs: have a big bankroll going in, play minimum on the pass line, the maximum allowed on the odds behind the pass line, continuous minimum come bets with maximum odds behind them, and just hope the dice run your way that night. Field bets, and any bets in the middle of the table where the dealers stand are for the Squares. Easy money, right?

Anyway, there's a reason for this craps diatribe. Eleven is a magic number in college basketball conference games. The bigger the underdog, the better chance we have at cashing the ticket.

SIDE HUSTLE

Since 2005, conference road dogs of 11 or more points do very well in the desert:

*Conference Road Dogs of 11 points or more in regular season
3534-3214-158, 52.4%

The 52.4% isn't far above the 52.38% needed to break even, but often these 11-point dogs have less juice than –110. As always, never bet a spread with any juice more than –110, because it makes things much more difficult to make a profit.

Pre-Conference Tournament Unders: At Thanksgiving and Christmas, we see a lot of college basketball tournaments. Whether it's in Hawaii, Alaska, or some other luxurious location, college programs travel all around the world to play tournaments at the holidays. But in these games, the unders have value since 2004:

*Unders on Neutral Courts in November and December
2228-1970-60, 53.1%

That's big 4,200+ game sample size from which to choose. Both teams playing in unfamiliar arenas where they probably will never play again in their careers. It's a recipe for underachieving offensively. So while most people are sitting around the holidays watching these games and rooting for points, we root against human achievement as per usual. And also, as per usual, the numbers back us up.

I can't drive 155! Our Sammy Hagar prop. Van Halen was better with David Lee Roth, and that isn't even up for debate, but I digress. But in college basketball, 155 is the magic number. If you see a total of 155 or more, regular or postseason, go under the total. Since 2005, you've made a nice profit in doing just that.

SIDE HUSTLE

Unders 155 or more
2425-2109-56, 53.5%

A sample size of over 4,500 games tells it all. When the desert tells you 2 teams are going to score big, go against it.

MLB

"You need a full bottle of whiskey and a revolver to sweat baseball." - Nick Bogdanovich, longtime sportsbook manager in Las Vegas

"Momentum? Momentum is the next day's starting pitcher" - Hall of Fame Manager Earl Weaver

"Baseball is like marriage, and football is like sex" - Brad Taylor

Bogdanovich said this once on a national VSiN show, and they made a t-shirt out of the phrase. There's a lot of truth to this statement from a guy like Bogdanovich, who has literally seen it all in the world of sports gambling. He's another guy who we should always take his opinions very seriously.

The 2nd quote here is an old school way of thinking about baseball. That works in MLB, but it no longer works for handicapping. We will discuss why Earl Weaver couldn't deal with today's game.

The 3rd quote isn't saying anything bad about the fine institution of marriage. But it's very true! Football games don't occur every day! Your favorite team, a concept we are against if you are a true sports gambler, plays once a week. In a usual fall week, we have one Thursday night NFL game, some college games sprinkled on a Friday night, and a full Saturday of college football, followed by NFL Sunday. Add in Monday Night Football and then take a couple of days off to get back to the real world. Ever listen to sports talk radio hosts complain about Wednesdays during the fall? It's the calm before the next storm of football to talk about. That's why the sports media sometimes must make mountains out of mole hills and blow things out of proportion to keep their ratings by appealing to the lowest common denominators who fall for such shenanigans.

But the theme of these quotes is the same: betting MLB is a grind. The length of the season will get to you because it's almost every day for 6 months from April to September, and then you have the playoffs which seems to expand every year!

And the "Adapt or Die" mentality reigns truer in MLB than any other sport. Gone are the days when old school manager Earl Weaver would say that momentum in MLB was simply the next day's starting pitcher. When I first started handicapping MLB, starting pitchers regularly lasted 6-7 innings. The best would easily go 8-9. Today, only the best pitchers go 6-7 innings, and most are lucky to go 5. The game has changed. Bullpen skill and usage is a very important handicapping tool, with the latter being more important. If a closer has pitched 2 consecutive games, or 3 out of 4, or 4 out of 5, they aren't likely to pitch in the next game. The best relief pitchers don't throw anywhere close to 80 innings anymore. It's somewhere in the 70's, which is less than 1 inning every 2 games.

Baseball is a different breed than the point spread wagers of football and basketball. It's the money line, where the bettor only needs to pick the winner. That makes the -110 juice/vig something we don't deal with in money line MLB wagers.

The first year I started watching baseball and realizing what was going on was 1977. In that season, Nolan Ryan and Jim Palmer each pitched 22 complete games. If a pitcher did that today, the manager would be thrown in jail for abuse! In 2022, The Marlins' Sandy Alcantara threw 6 complete games, and he won the Cy Young Award. But that was an obvious outlier. In each of the previous 4 seasons, no starting pitcher had thrown more than 3 complete games in a season. In fact, only 1 pitcher has thrown double digit complete games in a season this century (James Shields, 11 for Tampa in 2011. The game has changed. From The Nasty Boys (Norm Charlton, Rob Dibble, and Randy Myers) leading the Cincinnati Reds to a World Series in 1990, to the Kansas City Royals depending on a great bullpen (Kelvin Herrerra, Wade Davis, and Greg Holland) to take a franchise from nowhere to an AL Championship in 2014 and a World Series Championship in 2015. And as soon as those guys on both teams got too much age and mileage on them, those franchises went back to being less than mediocre. Coincidence?

Having said all that, I look to play mostly totals these days in MLB. Laying favorites of more than –150 is a quick recipe for disaster. So, we look mostly for totals we can take advantage of, while looking for the occasional dog.

Division Dogs (with an asterisk): Gone are the days (for now) when division rivals in MLB play 19 games against each other. Now, it's down to 12-13. While that's better for the fans, it's not better for us sports gamblers trying to take advantage of our beloved divisional dogs.

*Division Dogs of +138 through +155
918-1251-0, 42.3%   ROI 4.1%

With money line wagering in MLB, the juice matters that much more. Playing markets as we do, we look for divisional dogs from

+138 and +155. These teams get the added benefit of being division rivals and underdogs (both characteristics of value), but these teams aren't huge underdogs given no little chance of winning.

First Five Over Four!: Betting the "First Five" innings is much more reliant on the starting pitcher in today's game. The most common total in these First Five props are anywhere between 4.5 and 5.5 runs scored.

*Over in First 5 Innings for totals of exactly 4 with juice −110 or less 1595-1413-493, 53%

With totals of 4, you are getting good starting pitchers, and not the best. Or possibly, you're getting one great starting pitcher along with a mediocre one. Regardless, 4 is the magic number to go over in the First 5 innings. The public will see the big names of these great starting pitchers and assume nobody will score runs off them. Again, the numbers prove conventional wisdom to be crazy talk. As usual, make sure to watch the juice and not lay any odds more than −110.

Smokey and the Bandit 4: The Search For Coors!: One of the first movies I remember is Smokey and the Bandit. Burt Reynolds in a Trans Am with Jackie Gleason cursing like a sailor trying to catch him. Good times, indeed! The premise was that bad guys in Atlanta wanted Coors Beer, which for some reason was illegal to sell east of the Mississippi River in those days. Can you believe that? Marijuana and sports gambling is legal in most places now, and in the late 70's Coors Beer couldn't be found in the Eastern Time Zone! The times have changed for sure! Just watch those old Smokey and the Bandit movies from back in the day and see how the times were so much different than now!

SIDE HUSTLE

But Coors has been important in my life for different reasons. One of my favorite angles in baseball over the years, and especially rotisserie/fantasy baseball, has been The Rockie Shuffle. When Colorado entered MLB in the early 90's, Denver became a haven for hitters in the mile high thin air. Simultaneously, it was a death wish for pitchers. I cannot tell you how many fantasy baseball leagues I won by simply using a system called The Rocky Shuffle and filtering all Colorado hitters for their home at bats only. The Rocky Shuffle was obtaining as many players from Colorado as possible and utilizing them in all home games, while benching them on the road. The results were almost like playing video games! Three guys hit 40 HR for the Rockies in 1996 AND 1997. Larry Walker and Todd Helton played like Hall of Famers. Players like Ellis Burks, Charlie Hayes, Vinny Castilla, and Dante Bichette went from good baseball players to borderline superstars in their days with Colorado. Guys named Mike Kingery, Jeff Cirillo, and Jeffrey Hammonds did very little in their careers elsewhere but had superstar-quality seasons in Denver. From the 1995 to 2001 seasons, pitchers at Coors Field recorded an ERA of 6.50, more than two runs a game higher than the 4.37 ERA recorded at other stadiums. Something had to change, because it just wasn't fair that a thief like me could do something as simple as milking Colorado home games for boat loads of cash every year.

Then sadly, Colorado brought in The Humidor. I had gone about 2002 pre-baseball season with the belief that the money train was still running 81 times a year through Coors Field, and I was going to be on board once again for my share of the loot. Then they bring in the humidor before 2002, and the baseballs aren't flying nearly as far or as often as before. A few weeks into the season, I'm wondering what the heck is going on out there. Then TBS showed a Braves game in Colorado and showed a video of the humidor and what they did to baseballs. It was demoralizing because the party was over, but it was a lot of fun (and profitable) while it lasted. Coors Field is still the best hitting park in MLB, but not by anything close to the margin it was during the 90's and up to 2001. The Rocky Shuffle still exists, but just not to the level as before when even a schlep like me can see the home/road splits and take advantage of them. Each year to this day, I will check out the home/road splits of the Colorado hitters projected to start and hit in the top 6 of their lineup to start the season, and act accordingly. The Rocky Shuffle still works!

But the oddsmakers in the desert know this as well. They know the public sees those big numbers in the thin Colorado air and want to go over the total at all costs. But we have not one, but two systems we play involving totals at Coors Field, and they are very simple. Like conference road dogs in basketball, it's a "Yo, Eleven" play. Since 2005, Coors Field plays to the number 11.

*Unders in games at Coors Field with total of 11 or more
313-256-31, 55%
*Overs in games at Coors Field with total of 10.5 or less
459-376-21, 55%

Here are 2 systems in 1, all involving totals at Coors Field, that will give us action 81 games a season. Once again, the conventional wisdom says going over all the time at Coors Field is the play, but the numbers tell us another story. And once again, we are playing numbers and the market instead of starting pitchers and visiting teams. With a sample size of almost 1,500 games, 11 is the magic number in Denver.

SIDE HUSTLE

The Windy City, Harry Caray, and the 1984 Cubs: 1984 is considered one of the best years in sports history, and pop culture history for that matter. But for me, I wasn't very happy! I got a very bad hair style that made me a laughingstock amongst the people I knew. With that in mind, I stayed on the farm a little more than usual that summer, trying to comb my hair out every night until my hair grew up. It didn't work. Staying home all summer, I got to watch a lot more TV than usual as well. During the day in the summertime, it was the Chicago Cubs on WGN. Harry Caray would come on the air every day, talk crazy, have (more than) a few drinks, and talk even crazier. It was different than any baseball that was on TV in those days. And I started watching every day for entertainment. WGN started every game with Van Halen's "Jump," and the party went from there. The funny thing was that the Cubs were winning big! They eventually made the playoffs for the first time in decades. All their home games played in the daytime, an announcer who was beloved by everyone, and a team that never won. What could be better? The 1984 Cubs got me through the summer, only to do what the Cubs always did back then: lose in heartbreaking fashion to the Padres in the playoffs. Steve Garvey hasn't been so unlikeable since, unless you look at his private life, but I digress.

But just like the ball going through Leon Durham's legs, the Cubs broke their fans' hearts every year until finally winning in 2016. But it was 32 years too late! I had moved on from being a fan of this team, or any team. Speaking of Cubs' legends, remember Steve Bartman? The guy who tried to catch a foul ball, didn't, and gave the Marlins an extra out in Game 6 of the 2003 NLCS? Yeah, that guy. The Marlins scored 6 runs in the inning after Bartman did what he did, and Cubs fans everywhere blamed him for their team losing yet again. The reason I'm bringing up Bartman is because he pulled off the greatest disappearance act in history. Nobody has seen Bartman since that night in 2003. He was offered all kinds of money for interviews, and he was the most popular Halloween costume in 2003. Yet, no one outside his family and co-workers has seen him since that fateful night. David Copperfield couldn't disappear like this guy did, so Bartman deserves credit for pulling off something very few people in this world could: passing on fame and fortune. After the Cubs finally won the World Series, they team invited Bartman to Wrigley Field and got him a championship ring. He refuses. The guy won't budge.

Why are we talking about the Cubs so much? I get it, Side Hustle Guy! Kids of your generation watched the Cubs and Braves all summer and became fans into adulthood. But we grew up! Why the Cubs now? Wrigley Field! One of the smallest ballparks in MLB, conventional wisdom is that the "over" is the play most days in Cubs' home games. Heck, one time the Cubs lost a game at Wrigley by a score of 23-22! Somewhere in this world, there was a bettor who took the under in that game with 45 runs. That guy probably didn't have steak for dinner that night. But once again, conventional wisdom is dumb! Since 2005, 52.3% of games at Wrigley Field have gone under the total (727-663-68). That isn't enough to be a profitable system, but there's a reason why Chicago is called "The Windy City."

When the wind is blowing at Wrigley, it has a huge effect on the games. There are 2 systems we employ to take advantage of the wind here. First, the direction of the wind is very important. Sure, when the wind is blowing in, it's a big advantage for pitchers. But at Wrigley, with the configuration of the ballpark, the real advantage is when the wind is blowing "from right" field. Wait a minute, Side Hustle Guy! How do I know the direction of the wind? Go to any website that lists the lineups hours before games (mlb.com, espn.com, etc.). With those lineups, the wind direction and speed will also be listed. We will get to wind speed in a moment. But when the wind is blowing from right field, we can cash some tickets since 2005:

*Wrigley Field Unders when the wind is blowing "From Right Field"
139-102-13, 57.7%

Like any good informercial on at 3 AM yells, "and that's not all!" In games where the wind is blowing "in," look for totals of 7.5 or higher and go under.

Since 2005, this system also makes a nice profit:

*Wrigley Field Unders when wind is blowing "In" and total is 7.5 or higher
108-71-12, 60.3%

These aren't the biggest sample sizes we have in this book, but these are systems I look for 81 times a year for every Cubs home game. Yes, it takes a little hustle to check out the box score a couple hours before game time, but the juice is worth the squeeze.

Mea Kulpa!: Enrico Pallazzo

When I was in college, I was looking for ways to make money before I left for Atlanta. A friend of mine came up to me one day and said "Brad, I've got it! And you're perfect for this! We are going to be Little League umpires!" I looked at him like he was crazy! In a small town in central Kentucky, if I made one bad call on a kid, that family would never forgive me. And more importantly, that family would never forgive my parents either! So, while I was in Atlanta living it up, my poor family would be dodging some couple who thought I ruined their kid's potential MLB career by missing a call in Little League. Laugh if you want, but that stuff happens in small town

America! In other words, umpiring is a very difficult gig for many reasons!

And now, allow me to introduce you to a man named Ron Kulpa. He is our favorite MLB Umpire. OK, Side Hustle Guy, you're REALLY getting desperate now talking about the umpires! I disagree! If you are of the belief that umpires in MLB don't matter, then totals would be a coin flip, right? It doesn't matter who the umpire is, they are all equal and have the same tendencies and strike zones. Not a chance! Umpires matter. Want proof? Ron Kulpa is a big moneymaker as an umpire to go under the total since 2005:

*Unders when Ron Kulpa is home plate umpire
289-210-25, 57.9%

If umpires didn't matter, a guy like Kulpa would hit 50% overs and unders, not almost 58%. That's not coincidence. If you're one of those bettors who pays no attention to umpires, you're wrong. Until MLB brings in the computers to call balls and strikes, the umpires matter. And Kulpa is a great one for under bettors.

Another magic number: 11.5 is the magic number for MLB totals. Anytime you see a total of 11.5 or more, and it happens anywhere from 30-50 times per season for about the last decade.

SIDE HUSTLE

PART III

THE SPORTS BETTING CALENDAR

SIDE HUSTLE

SIDE HUSTLE

"I couldn't get a date from a calendar!" - Brad Taylor most of his life

Obviously, there's more sports on which we can wager than the 4 sports that we have addressed. Most of those sports are only worthy of our time for a few weeks, or even just one day per year. Although the basics remain the same for any sport (underdogs, under the totals, going against the public, looking for sharp money, etc.), some sports are entities all to themselves. Based on the time of year, sometimes our train of thought needs to change. In fact, I can always tell what time of year it is based on the types of bets I'm making.

With that in mind, another valuable portion of this book is our Sports Betting Calendar. What events do a sports bettor need to be handicapped based on the month of the year?

JANUARY

"Back to life, back to reality, back to the here and now." - Soul II Soul

Another homage to late 80's R&B, with maybe the best song beat you'll ever hear. How do I know it was good? Many songs I heard for the next 12-18 months after this song came out copied this song in some way, shape, or form. Imitation is the sincerest form of flattery.

January 2nd is a "Back to Life" kind of day that most people dread, but not me. One of my favorite days of the year is January 2nd for a few reasons: the holidays are finally over, college basketball conference schedules begin, and the NFL Playoffs are about to begin. Many will ask why I'm happy the holidays are over, and that's a problem for my therapist to talk about with me regarding my issues. But as a sports gambler who thrives on routine, getting back to the grind on January 2nd really helps the attitude and the bankroll, especially when Christmas sales and items are up in the big stores by August!

NFL PLAYOFFS

January means the NFL Postseason Tournament is underway. Again, we aren't looking to push the chalky favorites. It's the same old story. As much as the media tries to spin it otherwise, the NFL Playoffs is a microcosm of the regular season. We are looking to play underdogs and going under the total first and foremost.

BIG DOGS STILL RULE: Since we love underdogs in the NFL regular season, we must switch to favorites in the playoffs, right? Nope, we stick to the same principles. Underdogs are still the value play in postseason, covering 54.8% since 2003 (121-100-4). But the shorter the dog in the playoffs, the better the chance to cash the ticket. Dogs of 10 or less in the NFL Playoffs have done even better since 2003:

*Dogs in the NFL Playoffs of 10 points or less
116-90-4, 56.3%

Home, road, or neutral dogs all have about the same ATS win %, so we just like all dogs of 10 or less. The theory is that all these teams are playoff teams, so there's no weak links at this point.

DOGS BARK IN THE NFL PLAYOFFS, TOO!: Just like the first 3 weeks of the NFL regular season, the best time to play the dogs in the NFL Playoffs is the divisional round. This is when the great teams are sitting out, and the good teams are also playing good teams. Again, the difference between teams in the first round of the playoffs is miniscule. The proof is in the ATS results.

SIDE HUSTLE

*Dogs in NFL Playoffs Divisional Round
46-32-1, 59%

The difference between the teams facing off in the first round of the NFL Playoffs is miniscule, and it's proven by the fact that the underdogs cash so many tickets in the first week of elimination games.

THE GREAT OUTDOORS: I always thought Chevy Chase was a little overrated. He was great in Caddyshack, but so was everyone else in that movie. And that late night talk show lasted about 5 minutes before it was canceled, but I digress.

When we think of the NFL Playoffs, we think about games played outdoors in cold weather. NFL Films has made a legacy off telling stories of The Ice Bowl with Dallas and Green Bay in the 60's. I remember being a kid watching the 1981 Bengals-Chargers AFC Championship Game in what was the coldest game in NFL history and wondering how anyone could function in that weather, especially playing on that old school AstroTurf which was just a thin layer of carpet over thick concrete. We don't immediately think about playoff games played indoors, although many have been played there over the years.

But for our purposes, we look for bad weather. In the NFL Playoffs, all games since 2003 go under the total 52.3% of the time (116-106-4). But when those playoff games are played outdoors, the story changes. Since 2003, NFL Playoff games played outdoors with a total of 33.5 or more have made a nice profit in the desert.

*Under in NFL Playoff games played outdoors, total 33.5 or higher
98-74-4, 57%

The theory is that both teams facing off in these games are equal in performance, and both teams are playing "tight" with so much on the line. By January, the weather changes the game, and the betting line sometimes doesn't always catch up. With the added pressure of the NFL Playoffs, the under is a good bet in these situations, if the total isn't ridiculously low.

COLLEGE FOOTBALL PLAYOFF

Starting in 2024, the College Football Playoff will change. The format goes from 4 to 12 teams. In its current format, it's good news and bad news: the good news is underdogs are 5-3 in the 8 championship games of the College Football Playoff. The bad news is the favorites have won, covered, and dominated the first 3 National Championship Games in the 2020's. The sample sizes are not big enough to draw anything from this, but it's interesting the dogs covered the first 5, and didn't come close in the last 3.

In the current playoff format (before expansion), we haven't seen anything that we can identify as a system. This is mainly due to the fact that we don't have enough sample data.

National Semifinals: Dogs 8-10 ATS, Unders 11-7

National Championship Game: Dogs 5-4 ATS, Unders 2-7

TOTAL: Dogs 13-14, Unders 13-14

To date, these games have been a coin flip. And now with the new playoff format, and this crazy conference realignment on the horizon, anything goes.

The January non-College Football Playoff Bowl Games, like the late December bowl games, have become nothing other than a psychology test. Which team "wants the game more?" Is one team happy to be there and exceeded expectations? Did one team expect to make the Playoff and must settle for a New Year's Day Bowl? Is either quarterback sitting out and turning pro? Did the coach leave for a better job? It's one of those "read the tea leaves" deals like the NFL Draft, the NBA Draft, and the NFL Preseason.

BIG DOGS BARK IN THE NEW YEAR: The magic number is non-Playoff bowls is 4.5. Again, we play markets, not teams. But in this case, we have to play teams as well based on information. If a team in a January bowl game is an underdog of 4.5 points to 9 points, that team covers the spread 62.7% of the time since the 2004 season.

*Dogs in January Bowls of 4.5 to 9 points
42-25-0, 62.7%

With January bowls not called the College Football Playoff, we must do our homework and hustle. Look for motivational factors, coaching and quarterback availability, and become crack psychologists. But as always, look for the undervalued underdogs.

BOTTOM LINE:
January can be a month where we think things change in football, but they really only change in the colleges. The NFL Playoffs are almost a mirror of the regular season. While the college bowls look nothing like what we saw during the regular season. Keep in mind that many college football teams end their seasons in late November, then play their bowl games over a month later. A lot can change in a teenager's life in 5-6 weeks, including their performance on the field.

FEBRUARY

I often proclaim February 15th as one of my favorite days of the year. Sure, March and the NCAA Tournament are fast approaching, but it also means the fake observance of Valentine's Day is over. As a guy, the best advice I can give my fellow gentlemen on Valentine's Day is that you BETTER not skip this one. Even if your better half says something like "Oh, please! I don't want anything special! Please don't get me any flowers or candy for this Hallmark Holiday." Pay ABSOLUTELY no attention to this. It's a test, and it's a trick! Just play the game for one day and reap the benefits the next 364. Your entire life, not just your love life, will be much better off. This might be the best advice given in this entire book.

THE SUPER BOWL

February also means The Super Bowl. In the last 20 years, the public has been right 50% of the time in picking the right side ATS (10 out of 20). Underdogs are 13-7 ATS in the last 20 Super Bowls, and the under has hit 11 of the last 20. In other words, the playoffs mirror the regular season in terms of results in the desert.

A trick that I will use in the Super Bowl, which isn't really a trick, is when I figure out which team I'm picking to win. Then, look at the MVP odds for the winning team's quarterback. You'll be able to get better odds on the quarterback to win MVP than the team to win the game, and certainly to cover the spread. Quarterbacks won the MVP 32 out of the first 57 Super Bowls. If you think Team A is going to win the game, see what the odds are for that team's quarterback to win the MVP, and act accordingly.

PROP CULTURE: Super Bowl Props are always a big deal, especially to the media. During Super Bowl week, the Square media will go over the ridiculous props avaiable to bettors. We can thank William "The Refrigerator" Perry for starting this hysteria back when the 1985 Chicago Bears ruled the world. Perry was a huge defensive lineman for the Bears, who had scored a few touchdowns that regular season as part of Mike Ditka's revenge on San Francisco coach Bill Walsh running an offensive lineman against him the previous season. In sports talk radio, we enjoy discussing people who are bitter to the end. Ditka was one of the best at that, holding grudges forever! But William Perry had become one of the biggest names in America overnight, as a man at least 350 pounds running over people on national television. For the Super Bowl that year, Jimmy Vaccaro (a name we have mentioned already in this book) put up odds on whether Perry would score a touchdown in the game at 20-1. The public pounced on this, and by game time the odds were down to 2-1. Vaccaro and all the Vegas books who posted odds on Perry scoring lost their tails when Perry got into the end zone (while Hall of Fame running back Walter Payton did not). At that moment, Super Bowl props were born.

Super Bowl props are now an industry in itself. As soon as the length of the national anthem is set, bettors immediately go to YouTube and find examples of that artist to see their average time compared to the time the oddsmakers set. I don't play many props for the Super Bowl. If I do, I'm looking to go under totals for yardage or receptions for certain players. Not only has the newness worn off the props, but so has the value. With all props, make sure to check out the juice/vig on them. Anything more than –110 juice/vig should be looked at very carefully and cautiously.

For February, I'm concerned about college basketball conference games, looking for big road dogs more than anything else. As for the Super Bowl, look to fade the public. Otherwise, it's Amateur Hour for those of us who have been grinding football games for almost 6 months.

MARCH

There isn't a better day of the year than NCAA Tournament Selection Sunday. Not only have we finally survived the long, cold winter, but we also get the bonus of moving our clocks forward an hour! It can get demoralizing in the middle of Winter when it gets dark so early. But Selection Sunday is the unofficial beginning of Spring, and easily my favorite day of the year. Sure, we move the clocks up, but we also get our grubby hands on those wonderful brackets.

It's all about the NCAA Tournament and nothing else matter in March, right? Wrong, again! Here's a little secret: the Sharps play the Conference Tournaments more than the NCAA Tournament. More games and rivalries with rematches (and in some cases, 3rd matchups), make for a week that has more opportunities for cashing tickets than the NCAA Tournament, if that's possible.

Regardless of the tournament, here are my favorite systems in March:

MARCH MADNESS! The Missouri Valley Conference Tournament is always one of those tournaments that few people pay attention to annually. The finals of this tournament have always been played on the Sunday BEFORE Selection Sunday, 7 days before the brackets are announced. While the Power 5's play their tournaments, the MVC has already finished is sitting around waiting.

*MVC Tournament unders
108-63-0, 63.2%

SIDE HUSTLE

The best news about this tournament is that it's played in the same arena in St. Louis every season. That's what makes this system so consistently good every season. No matter the round of this tournament, the unders make a profit. We hope nothing ever changes in the Missouri Valley, and hopefully neither does the low scoring games in their tournament.

ELITE 8 DOGS: The NCAA Tournament is an event in which the public loves to wax poetic about the underdogs. We all remember the huge upsets. But when we look at the numbers, the underdogs aren't a big moneymaker ATS. In fact, there's only one round in the NCAA Tournament where the underdogs turn a profit enough to blindly play each year. The Elite 8 round is the best for underdogs since 2005.

*Dogs in NCAA Tournament Elite 8
42-28-2, 60%

Blindly playing all the dogs will only lead to a lighter bankroll, despite how CBS tries to spin everything into a Cinderella Story where the underdogs always pull off the upsets. The desert makes sure reality always wins out over fantasy.

THE HEAT IS ON! Glenn Frey never made a huge splash once he left the Eagles, but he was part of 2 legendary 80's soundtracks: Beverly Hills Cop, for this reference to The Heat Is On, and Miami Vice. Nothing was cooler in the mid 80's than Miami Vice and Eddie Murphy. Of course, the Eagles said after they broke up that they'd get together when Hell Freezes Over. In 1994, after all of their solo careers were busted, Hell Froze Over and the Eagles had the #1 Album in America for the year.

SIDE HUSTLE

In March, the heat is always on. But it's especially on during the tournament final games, and both teams know it.

*Unders in Conference and Postseason Tournament Finals
327-254-12, 56.3%

This is one of my favorite March systems. When it's the finals of any tournament, from NCAA Championship to your favorite Cupcake Conference, go under the total.

DANA RULES: Something I didn't know before researching this book was that Queen Latifah's real first name is Dana. I guess I thought her first name really was "Queen."

But the real Dana in the month of March is Dana Altman of Oregon. Much like we love Tony Bennett of Virginia in the regular season, we love Altman in the postseason. From the Pac-12 Tournament to the NCAA Tournament, Altman cashes tickets at a crazy level in his career with the Ducks:

*Dana Altman Postseason ATS at Oregon
42-22-3, 65.6%

We don't think of Bennett and Altman among the very best coaches in America. But I can assure you that the desert does, especially when Oregon hits the postseason. Just like the more famous Dana, that's why the point spread is the real Equalizer.

We didn't forget about you, KenPom: When we think of underdogs in the NCAA Tournament, do we think of teams that run up and down the court at full speed. Well, other than the 1990 Loyola Marymount team. That was another story altogether. But upsets and unexpected close games are usually by teams that slow the game down and shorten the game. Heck, I do that in Tecmo Bowl against my friends who were much more talented than me at the game. It would upset them that I would pull my stunts and shorten then game, giving myself a chance at the end to win when they were the better player. It's the same concept by looking at pace of play in the NCAA Tournament.

The system is easy. Look for underdogs, then go visit our pal KenPom and look for those dogs who average 73 possessions per game or less. Simply doing that cashes tickets in The Tournament:

*NCAA Tournament Dogs averaging 73 possessions per game or less
362-304-14, 54.4%

Slow paced underdogs are gold in the Tournament.

DEFENSE DOESN'T SLUMP: When a team puts up a big defensive effort in the NCAA Tournament, it often rolls into the next round. The magic number here is 56. When a team allows 56 points or less in the Tournament, and they're a dog in the next round, that dog often barks:

*NCAA Tournament Dogs that allowed 56 points or less in previous round
80-46-1, 63.5%

This is one of my favorite systems. I know I'm getting a defensive oriented dog in the Round of 32 or later. Those teams are golden ATS, as seen by their winning percentage.

SIDE HUSTLE

BOTTOM LINE

March is my favorite sports gambling month, but there are more opportunities in conference tournaments than the NCAA Tournament. Act accordingly!

APRIL

MLB EARLY 2-STEP: In fantasy baseball, weekly leagues often refer to starting pitchers who start 2 times in a 1-week scoring period as a "2-stepper." Simple math can help you determine that a starting pitcher with 2 starts has a better chance of picking up a win and several more strikeouts than a pitcher that starts only once. Then again, a bad 2-stepper can kill your ERA. But that's another story for another day.

For our purposes here, 2-steppers are very important to start the season. Most MLB teams want to begin the season well by giving their ace starting pitcher the opening day. But chaos and anarchy happen starting with Game 2 of the season. In Game 2, the starters aren't as good, and maybe the closers and back end of the bullpens are already being used a little too much, especially to start a season with the same workload as per usual in terms of rest and usage. Starting with Game 2, and going through almost 2 turns in each team's starting rotation, the road dogs bark the loudest!

*Road Dogs in Games 2-9 of regular season
301-389-0, 43.6%   ROI 13.6%

You can see that the numbers here are only 43.6% winners. But with money line wagering, these underdogs cash in big! That's why there's a 13.6 ROI in picking these early season dogs. The theory here is that past each team's ace, the desert doesn't know nearly as much about each team's 2-5 spots in the starting rotation. And while the best pitchers are good annually, the mediocre ones can be up and down. The odds in April aren't nearly as tight or as accurate in the first couple of weeks as they will be in the summertime. This is the best time for the road dogs in MLB: Early!

EARLY SEASON DIVISION ROAD DOGS: Our favorite teams in any professional sports are the divisional road dogs or conference road dogs in the colleges. But with MLB being a different sport bet mainly on the moneyline, it makes for a different way of approaching the sport. We do like the divisional road underdogs, but only in the first portion of the season. The historical data says we can make a profit off this since 2005:

Division Road Dogs Games 2-36 of season
1493-1890-0, 44.1%   ROI 3.2%

Going blindly with division dogs doesn't work for the entire season, but it works early. The oddsmakers make much tighter lines once they have a couple of months of data from which to gather. That means Squares like us can capitalize early with divisional road dogs. Play these teams in the first quarter of the season.

NFL DRAFT

Ah, yes. The NFL Draft. Ever since Mel Kiper first appeared on ESPN in the early 80's, every NFL fan thinks they can draft better than any NFL General Manager. And now, you can put your money where your mouth is! NFL Draft Props have become a huge deal out in the desert. In fact, the oddsmakers in the desert despise putting up odds on the NFL Draft. Why? Because the public has been winning!

The NFL Draft and NBA Draft have nothing to do with handicapping games. It's information based. Can you discern the correct information? Do you trust certain "Draft Experts" and distrust others? The desert puts limits on Draft Props, but if the bettor has the information, that bettor can do very well.

As we covered earlier, the NFL Draft can be profitable by following the right information and the late money.

THE MASTERS

Every Spring, people get Golf Fever! And the first PGA Major is The Masters. Living in Atlanta, it was less than an hour to Augusta, Georgia. But Augusta is just another small southern town 51 weeks out of the year. It's that 52nd week that puts this community on the map. And the course is like going back in time: cheap concessions, tickets are impossible to get, no running on the golf course, and the same people sit in the same places year after year. But don't be fooled! Augusta National pulls all the strings on everything the public sees, and they do it better than anyone. The control they have is amazing, and the golf world just bows to their every want. Why? Because as we say, it's all about who you are in life. But they really don't have to add the artificial bird noises to the CBS telecast, though (they do!).

Betting golf has also become a big deal, especially live in-game wagering. There are all kinds of ways to bet on golf: who wins the tournament, Top 5/10/20 wagers, over/under on scoring for the tournament and individual players. When I venture into the world of golf betting, it's only with player matchups. In these matchups, the oddsmakers will put 2 players together and all you must do is select the player who will get the better score between those two only. It's a safer bet than picking Player A at crazy odds to win the tournament and defeat everyone in the field.

SIDE HUSTLE

The Masters is the best major to bet as a handicapper for one reason: this tournament is played on the same course every year. While the other majors are played on different courses each year, a "defending champion" isn't really defending a title if they aren't even playing on the same course! With The Masters, and most golf tournaments played on the same course for that matter, the stat "Average Strokes Gained" is a basic number that will help any beginning or experienced handicapper pick winners of tournaments played on the same courses annually.

Joe Peta, who wrote a GREAT book about MLB betting in 2013 called Trading Bases. Peta approached betting baseball like we do by betting markets and numbers, not teams and people. But Peta also ventured into the world of golf handicapping a few years ago when he wrote a book about The Masters, and golf handicapping. I've never met Joe Peta, but I'm a big fan of his material. If you are into golf betting I recommend looking into his work, first and foremost.

MAY

NBA PLAYOFFS

Wait a minute, why haven't I seen anything to this point about the NBA? In keeping track of my best, being self-aware, and playing to my strengths, I no longer wager NBA regular season. But the playoffs, are a different story totally. No more Load Management. No more silliness. They're all playing for the money now.

EARLY FAVORITES: Favorites in the First Round of the NBA Playoffs do very well over the years. Since 2005, the numbers speak for themselves:

*Favorites in First Round of NBA Playoffs

SIDE HUSTLE

438-369-20, 54.3%

It's not something to play after the First Round when the series become more competitive. But early, this has been a solid play regardless of matchups.

THE ZIG ZAG THEORY! An old school favorite! One of the most tried and true systems in the NBA Playoffs. It's simple: just wager on the team that lost the previous game. For years in the 80's and 90's, this system worked very well. Recency Bias would rule, and fans that just saw Team A win the previous game would think there's no way Team B can win the next one. And the odds would always jump towards the team that won the previous game. Eventually, bettors figured out that going to opposite way of that Conventional Wisdom often cashed the tickets. And oddsmakers eventually caught up too. Now, you see the point spread worse for the team that lost the previous game. Again, if schleps like us know about The Zig Zag, everybody does. And since 2005, if you played The Zig Zag Theory blindly, you'd be losing money by cashing only 50.3% of the time (719-710-28). But we still see a Zig Zag angle that still works:

*First Half NBA Playoffs Home Dogs that lost previous game straight up
121-92-7, 56.8%

We are playing the first half line in this one and getting a desperate home team. This is the final remnant of the Zig Zag Theory that still cashes in over long periods of time.

UNDER PRESSURE: Too bad Queen stole that song from Vanilla Ice, and Suge Knight. Oh well, like college basketball tournament finals, teams tighten up late in NBA Playoff series. In Games 6 and 7 since 2005, the numbers back that up.

*NBA Playoffs Unders in Games 6-7
130-88-0, 59.6%

Here's my favorite NBA Playoff system, just waiting on the players and coaches to stress out and think too much. My kind of system.

THE KENTUCKY DERBY

Ah, yes. The Run for the Roses, first Saturday in May. Growing up in central Kentucky, the horse racing capital of the world, the Derby is a big deal. Heck, horse racing is a big deal. Keeneland is just a stone's throw.

Kentucky Derby (Horse Racing): Back in olden times (the mid 20th Century), the 3 biggest sports in America were Horse Racing, Boxing, and Major League Baseball. Needless to say, that isn't the case now. But that doesn't stop people from trying to pick a winner in the Kentucky Derby every year.

And as someone who grew up in Central Kentucky, the horse racing capital of the world, I knew all about playing the horses. And so did all the people I knew growing up. Well, at least we thought we knew what we were doing. Spoiler Alert: we didn't. Of course, most of the people I knew couldn't read the program or racing form that gave out all the information about a horse and they just bet on the horse's name or number on the horse more than anything else. Those are always quick ways to go home broke!

Consistently winning against the horses is a VERY tough proposition. It's pari-mutuel wagering, which is another way of saying that all the bettors are betting against themselves. The more money that comes in on a horse, the odds will move immediately. And unlike regular sports wagering, the tracks hold more than 20%. Can you honestly say that you know someone who makes a consistent profit at the tracks? If you do, please give me the number of that person so they can help me!

So, although I am a kid who grew up running at tracks like Keeneland, The Red Mile, and even Churchill Downs, I'm certainly not a horse racing expert. Once I ran the numbers, I realized it just isn't possible to win long term, especially someone like me who doesn't follow horse racing other than The Triple Crown races and maybe Breeder's Cup races. Don't forget, I am a sports talk radio host in Lexington, Kentucky, so I am surrounded by this and still only pay attention a few times a year. But for one race annually, like the Kentucky Derby, there's nothing wrong with a little pizza money on the line. Looking at jockeys, trainers, closing speed, breeding, and recent results can help handicap the race, but it should be for nothing more than a pizza money bet to have some action on Derby Day. Because as we know, one bet shouldn't change your life, especially in The Sport of Kings.

SIDE HUSTLE

JUNE
NHL PLAYOFFS

"I'm gonna make Gretzky bleed!" - Vince Vaughn in Swingers

Talking about guys playing video games earlier always goes back to this scene in the movie *Swingers* when Vince Vaughn and his friends were playing Blades of Steel before going out on the town. Of course, his opponent was wearing a Wayne Gretzky #99 jersey at the time. As a guy, there comes a time in a young man's life when you stop wearing the jerseys and stop turning the hats around backwards. Then again, I was that guy in the arcade in the early 80's that played with Russia on that arcade game with the USA vs Russia that nobody would play unless they had the USA. I enjoyed hitting that crowd noise "boo" button relentlessly on that game just to annoy my opponent. Go figure!

For once glorious spring and early summer of 1994, I started to become interested in the NHL. The New York Rangers had finally won a Stanley Cup (they haven't won since), and the entire playoffs were shown on ESPN. I dare say the NHL was as popular in this country as it had ever been, and then the players went on strike to start the next season. Heck, the NHL once missed an ENTIRE season once due to a strike. Just think if the NFL did that! They wouldn't be that crazy.

I don't watch hockey anymore. I probably knew more about it when I religiously watched ESPN SportsCenter decades ago than I do now. But just like the NBA Playoffs, we look to go under the total in Game 7 of any series in the NHL Playoffs. If you've done that since 2006, you've cashed 61.2% of your tickets (41-26-9). Otherwise, I'll keep my hockey to video games going forward.

SIDE HUSTLE

NBA DRAFT

We addressed the Woj Bomb changing the entire 2022 NBA Draft earlier. This is much like the NFL Draft: discern the reliable information and look for the late money. Somebody has to make money off these drafts, so it needs to be us!

WIMBLEDON

Ah, yes. Wimbledon! Nothing ruined your game shows and soap operas in the summertime back in the day like Breakfast at Wimbledon. Tennis is another sport that has a niche gambling audience. Those who follow it will swear by it, and swear they are making money betting it. I haven't followed tennis closely since the days of Connors and McEnroe, which means a very long time! The biggest gripe I hear among tennis bettors is that anytime a player retires, all bets can be canceled regardless of where the match is when it ends. I am not an expert at tennis, but it's a sport that seemingly can be profitable for those that follow closely. If you're looking for a fringe sport that seemingly has action the entire calendar year, here is your chance!

WNBA, CFL, and EPL

Here are some other Summertime sports that have their niche sports gambling audiences. I will admit that I have never wagered a WNBA game, but we can equate it to betting a smaller conference in college basketball. Not in terms of anything on a male/female debate, but in terms of betting action. There are 12 WNBA teams, and a sports bettor could find systems to play that league. I simply don't. Having said that, if I ever had the time and historical data, I'm sure coming up with some WNBA systems could be profitable.

SIDE HUSTLE

The CFL has been around forever. I remember Warren Moon and Doug Flutie ruling that league way back when we first got ESPN and that's the only professional football they could show for a long time. The CFL currently has 9 teams. Which means 1 team is always left out in the cold. Get it? Canada? Left out in the cold? Oh well. I'd rather drive myself crazy with MLB totals than get started in another sport that I haven't followed for decades.

English Premiere League (EPL) soccer is the biggest sports league in the world outside of the USA. In England, where they've been able to bet on sports forever, it's their biggest gambling event. Ironically, they bet a lot on American Politics, but that's another story for another day. I never grew up watching or playing soccer, so I don't bet it either. I do know that the same rules apply for these sports mentioned here like the other sports: don't lay more than –110 juice, look to take dogs, look to go under totals, and look to play the markets. Since it feels like every soccer game ends 1-0 anyway, going under totals shouldn't be a problem!

JULY

"Vacation, all I ever wanted." The Go-Go's

My favorite schoolteacher is always more fun on June 1st than August 1st. Summertime is here! But in July, it's time for my vacation. The MLB All-Star Game is here, and that's my week off from everything. Turn off the lights, turn on the big, loud fan, and let me sleep for a week!

Although no sports are going on other than MLB, July could be the most important month of a sports bettor's calendar year. It's a time to look back and reflect on how you've performed over the previous year. It's a good time to change your minimum wager also. If you've been winning, you can cash out and remain wagering the same amount. Or you can increase your wagers to the same percent of your bankroll you were wagering before the Summer break. Once I look at my results, I don't change my wager size for an entire calendar year until the following July.

Also, it's a time to look at what type of bets you made money on from the previous year, and what bets forced you to eat ramen noodles instead of steaks. For those bets you performed poorly, look to change them by changing your handicapping style, or just crossing them off your list completely.

The MLB All-Star Break in July is the absolute perfect time of year to reassess your wagering from the previous year and act or change accordingly. Adapt or die!

AUGUST
NFL PRESEASON

"Off a guy who will be bagging groceries in a couple of weeks." - Manager Lou Brown after Willie Mays Hayes demonstrates newfound power hitting in Spring Training, Major League 2

For me, August is a great month. The weather is still hot, and football season is on the way. A nationally televised MLB game between teams in a pennant race won't get half the viewers of an NFL Preseason game. The NFL is king, even in August. So can we make money off these games? Someone is, so why can't it be us?

Once again, pay no attention to the haters. The ones who tell you that betting NFL Preseason is a sign of having a serious problem. If that was the case, how come the desert limits how much you can bet on these games? During the regular season, you can bet as much as you want on any NFL game. Why are they limited in the preseason? Think about that.

And this is the only time of year that coaches will tell you what they play to do. Will the starters play into the 2nd half? Will the starters play at all? Who are the backup quarterbacks and how much will they play? By the way, looking at the quarterback depth chart can help with preseason handicapping by knowing who will be playing at the end of these games. You don't get anything like that in the regular season. Like Michael Larson of Press Your Luck, take advantage of what the game gives you.

But don't get fooled by what you see in the NFL Preseason. When I moved to Atlanta in 1990, all I could watch was the local TV channels. In fact, I used aluminum foil and wire hangers to help with reception. The channel I picked up best just happened to be the channel that broadcast all the Falcons preseason games. What a break! What I saw that preseason over 4 weeks was something incredible. Jerry Glanville was in his first year in Atlanta, and he was bringing in the "Run N' Shoot" offense: 4 wide receivers, 1 running back, and lots of passing. That preseason, the Falcons looked like world beaters! They went 4-0, scored a league high 127 points, and no team had a better point differential. They looked like a combination of the 1999 Rams offensively and the 1985 Bears defensively. I couldn't believe that the nation wasn't seeing what I was seeing!

In 1990, I had my first fantasy football draft with friends I had made in school. But as we entered that fantasy draft, nobody was discussing the elephant in the room. ALL of us had seen the Falcons preseason games. Suddenly, every Falcon with a pulse was getting drafted WAY ahead of where they should be going in a draft. Newcomer Andre Rison was a first-round pick, and he wound up having a very good season. Quarterback Chris Miller was drafted like he was Dan Marino in his prime. And other Falcons skill players were being drafted like they were stars, all off 4 preseason games. I also remember that my first 2 picks in my first fantasy football league were Warren Moon and Thurman Thomas. I did just fine that year.

As the season started, the Falcons took on Glanville's old team, the Houston Oilers. And Atlanta buried them in Fulton County Stadium on that day. I remember watching that game on television thinking after a 4-0 preseason and putting up 47 points on a very good Oilers team, this team was winning big in 1990! Well, I was dead wrong. The Falcons only won 2 of their next 13 games. In other words, what we see in the summertime means absolutely nothing once the games mean something. From that point forward, I never placed any value on NFL Preseason results.

But that doesn't mean we can't bet these games! In fact, history tells us we are crazy if we don't.

JOHN HARBAUGH, KING OF AUGUST: Are certain teams covering or not covering point spreads in the preseason just a coincidence? Don't tell that to the Ravens! John Harbaugh has been nothing short of incredible in August since becoming coach of Baltimore:
*Baltimore Ravens in Preseason under John Harbaugh
38-16-1, 70%

Doesn't matter if they are a favorite, underdog, on the road, at home, or who starts at quarterback. John Harbaugh cashes tickets like no other. If you think better preseason games is silly, that's fine. More money for me.....

SHORT ROAD DOGS RULE EVEN IN AUGUST: The myth of the 3-points the desert adds to teams for being at home is even more advantageous for us in the NFL Preseason. Since 2004, the preseason short road dogs look a lot like the regular season short road dogs:

*Preseason Road Dogs of 3 points or less
287-238-19, 54.7%

Nobody knows about these preseason games, so why not take the short road dogs? History tells us it's the right side.

37 IS THE MAGIC NUMBER: Surely, the unders don't hit in the preseason like the regular season. And please, don't call me Shirley. But anytime a preseason game has a total of 37 points or more since 2004, the under keeps cashing the tickets:

*NFL Preseason Unders of 37 points or more
354-266-12, 57.1%

In addition, playing the over when the total is less than 37 also cashes big!

*NFL Preseason Overs of 36.5 or less
274-221-7, 55.4%

This is well over 1,000 games of sample size! What more proof do you need? Let them insult you for playing silly NFL Preseason games. I play these games annually, and the numbers say you should too.

FANTASY FOOTBALL

I don't discuss this a lot, even on the radio, but I wrote for Fantasy Football Index Magazine for about a decade back in the 90's and 2000's. It was a labor of love at the time, and it was also a great precursor to being a sports talk radio host. One time, I recommended Ricky Williams as a Top 5 running back for a particular week. Williams was injured very early in the game, and a fan emailed me saying "Great pick on Ricky Williams, loser!"

My response was quick and simple: "I apologize for not being able to predict injuries. Thanks for reading the column. Good luck!"

There will always be naysayers. There will always be Monday Morning Quarterbacks. There will always be those who are smarter than you. Well, at least they think they are. Every single time I made a mistake in life, regardless of my age or the circumstance, my father would always remind me of how stupid he thought I was. On the farm it was "Boy, you don't use your head," when I did something that wasn't up to his unrealistic expectations. Expectations, huh? Where have we heard that before.

But my favorite one-liner my dad always gave "I knowed it." Every time he said that to me, it was comforting. That sounds crazy, I know. But knowing that he was using the wrong form of speech in saying "knowed" reminded me that he wasn't exactly a genius himself. Emmitt Smith became an NFL commentator on ESPN after his career and used the word "knowed" several times. After one season, Smith was politely let go by ESPN.

But have you ever noticed that these people never step out on a limb? They refuse to enter the arena, other than from their computer. And that's fine. But I learned very early on in this racket, that is you pay attention to the crowd, you will soon become one of them. And unlike most, I like to stand out from the crowd. Those are the people who do special things in this world.

With sports gambling becoming more prominent in the country, fantasy football isn't as big as it used to be. People don't want to draft a team, play it out for 17 weeks, then finally crown a champion. We don't live in that world anymore. Songs on the radio now last less than 3 minutes, not 8 like in the classic rock days. We all have attention deficit disorder when it comes to everything.

Fantasy football is nothing like when I first played in 1990. Back then it was about 2 things: information and crunching numbers. People who didn't have the information was at a disadvantage, but people who didn't numerically know each player's numerical draft value based on projections and the league's scoring system was at an even bigger disadvantage. Those days are over. We all have the same information now. The playing field is even. It's more of a crap shoot than ever. That's why I don't play nearly as much as I used to play, although fantasy football draft day is always fun. Sadly, this isn't about fun anymore. We are trying to make a profit.

SIDE HUSTLE

SEPTEMBER
NFL

NFL DOGS BARK LOUDEST IN SEPTEMBER: We love road underdogs in the NFL, but the best time to take them is in the first 3 weeks of the season. We don't know what to make of some of these teams early, and often we overreact to one or two early games. The proof is in the results since 2003:

> *Road Dogs in Weeks 1-3
> 301-254-16

The more data we have on these teams, the tighter these lines get. Until the betting public catches up, blindly playing all underdogs in the first 3 weeks has been a proven moneymaker in a sample size of over 500 games.

OCTOBER
MLB PLAYOFFS

With the new MLB Playoff setup, dogs have dominated in the early years. There's no reason to think that will change anytime soon.

HOME DOGS BARK LOUDLY!: The MLB Playoffs are different now. When I was growing up, 4 teams made the postseason. Now, it's up to 12! And the home dogs dominate the early rounds.

> *Home Dogs in ALCS/NLCS and ALDS/NLDS
> 64-51-0, 55.7%   ROI 19.8%

With money line wagering, we are getting even more bang for our underdog buck. That almost 20% ROI speaks for itself.

SIDE HUSTLE

NOVEMBER
COLLEGE FOOTBALL

MACtion is SATISFACTION!: What's a sign that football season is coming to an end, and the holidays are approaching? The MAC Conference begins playing games on Tuesday and Wednesday nights. ESPN loves these games. And so do the gamblers, especially if they are on the road dogs in these games.

*Road Dogs in November MAC games played on Tuesday and Wednesday
68-46-2, 59.6%

Over 110 games of sample, and almost 60% winners. That's enough for me. Don't be afraid to take MACtion road dogs once the calendar hits November.

PUT IT IN NEUTRAL (COURT):

College basketball gets going in November. And before you know it, there's holiday tournaments everywhere for Thanksgiving. It's a great time for these college teams to underperform on the scoreboard since 2005.

*Unders on Neutral Courts in November
1617-1397-41, 53.6%

Teams with new players, on the road playing another team with new players, and neither team has probably ever played at the neutral site. And with a 3,000-game sample size, going under in these Thanksgiving holiday tournaments hasn't been a turkey!

DECEMBER
COLLEGE FOOTBALL

CONFERENCE CHAMPIONSHIP GAMES

First Saturday in December usually means Power 5 championship games in college football. But history doesn't give us much of a picture of sides to take. Whether it's taking the dogs, fading the public, or any filter we can think of, we don't see much of an advantage here. Granted, we have small sample sizes because each conference plays one game a year.

EARLY BOWL GAMES

Enjoy these while you can! No telling what happens to these December bowl games with conference realignment and an expanded playoff. But as long as we have what we have, we can still cash some tickets.

The really big December bowl dogs bark very loudly. Any line over a full possession, and it pays off to take that dog!

*December Bowl Dogs of 8.5 or more
57-37-0, 60.6%

Even trying to figure out if a team cares about a bowl or not doesn't matter when they are getting such "disrespect" in the desert by being such a big underdog. And history says they are profitable as well.

NFL

SIDE HUSTLE

DECEMBER DIVISION UNDERS: As stated earlier, we love to take Division Unders when the total is 41 or more. But when the calendar turns to December, don't even worry about the 41. Just take all Division Unders since 2003!

*Unders in December Division Games
331-263-15, 55.7%

The weather is cold, the games are between division rivals late in the season, and that spells defense and conservative game play.

SIDE HUSTLE

CONCLUSION

What did we learn?

On every radio show that I do, I end each episode with "What did we learn on The **Bottom Line** today?" I then proceed to sound like a crazy person making up silliness to add to what I actually discussed. When I was in school, I had a teacher tell me that when writing follow this outline: Tell them what you're going to tell them, tell them, then tell them what you told them. Makes sense! I do that on all my radio shows daily.

What did we learn in this book? Other than I like 1980's R&B music:
- Sports gambling is difficult. You probably won't win unless you are disciplined in every aspect of handicapping.
- Money Management means everything. Never let one bet change your life, and never bet more than 5% of your bankroll at one time (I never bet more than 1%).
- Play this as a marathon, not a sprint.
- It takes work to think and bet like a Sharp instead of a Square.
- Lean towards taking underdogs and under totals a vast majority of the time.

SIDE HUSTLE

- Play the markets and systems, not people and teams.
- Keep track of your bets and pay attention to history.
- Look to play lines with –110 juice/vig or less.
- Develop a daily routine and work it without fail, regardless of the distractions in your life.
- Fade the public AKA media as often as possible.
- Trust the numbers and the data over clichés and The Eye Test.
- Surround yourself with positive people who will tell you the truth and not make you delusional.
- Keep reasonable expectations and a daily enthusiasm even during the bad times.
- Don't feel like you have to be a sports expert and watch every game. You don't.
- Be ready for opportunity when it knocks, because there is no warning.
- Remember that the oddsmakers in the desert know more than us. Respect their numbers because they are right.
- Stay away from overpriced parlays and teasers.
- Betting systems work, but only if used correctly.
- Take what the game gives you by maximizing signup bonuses and shopping around for the best odds.
- You are smart enough to handicap your own games, not pay others to do it for you.
- Be strong mentally and take risks. Play to your strengths by being self-aware.
- Don't let losing affect your relationships with family and friends.
- When you win, act like you've been there before.

BOTTOM LINE

That's it! Hopefully, with this book you can go from Square to Sharp. It takes a minute, but it can be done. But this is called "gambling." It's not called "guaranteed winning." You must work your **Side Hustle** every day. So until the next time, as always, may the winners be yours.....

SIDE HUSTLE

GLOSSARY

Action - A bet or wager. In MLB (Major League Baseball), bets can be made based on the starting pitchers, or just "action" meaning the starting pitchers mean nothing with the bet.

Against the spread or ATS- The result of a game including the point spread.

Back Door Cover – An underdog getting a meaningless score late in the game after the game has already been decided that covers the point spread for the underdog.

Bad Beat - A bet that looks like the bettor is going to win but doesn't. Everybody has stories of these, and nobody likes to hear them.

Bettor – You and me, trying to cash a ticket.

Board – A list of all games available for a sports bettor.

Bridge Jumper – Sports bettors that lay big money on big favorites on the moneyline. When those big favorites lose, they're looking to jump off a bridge.

Chalk - The favorite in a game.

SIDE HUSTLE

Chalk Pusher – Someone who likes to play nothing but favorites, often leading to losing long term.

Consensus - Team with most bets in a game over all sports books.

Contrarian – Someone who goes against conventional wisdom and succeeds. And something we strive to be daily.

Cover - The betting outcome on a point spread bet. For a favorite to cover, it must win by a number higher than the spread. An underdog can cover by losing by a number less than the spread or by winning the game outright.

Edge – The books have an edge over the bettor before each wager. That's why we have to hit 52.38% winners at –110 and betting the same amount each game just to break even.

Even (Even Money) - A $100 bet to win $100.

Exotic Bets – Everything that's not a straight bet. Parlays, teasers, and prop bets. In horse racing, everything other than a win, place, or show bet.

Favorite - A team favored to win a game.

Future bets - A bet on events that will happen further in the future like who will win a division or who will win a championship well in advance.

Handle - The total amount of money wagered on a game.

SIDE HUSTLE

Handicapping - Researching sports statistics to pick winners.

Hedging - Betting opposite of a previous bet to guarantee winning at least a small amount of money. This should be done on a person-by-person basis. There is no right or wrong answer most times with hendging.

Hook - A half-point in the spread

House – The books that take the bets, and who have an advantage over the bettors.

In-game wagers - Bets made after a game started.

Juice AKA The Vig- A commission books win on each bet. Most of the time, a bettor needs to put up $11 to win $10 on a straight bet against the point spread.

Limit - The maximum allowed wager on a single bet.

Lock - A large favorite, or a "guaranteed" win by a tout.

Long Shot - A big underdog.

Money line bet - A bet made if a team will win or lose outright with no point spread.

Nickel - A $500 bet.

SIDE HUSTLE

No Action - A game that is no longer taking bets and all wagers are refunded.

Oddsmaker - Someone who sets the opening line on a game. We refer to them as "the desert" quite a bit.

Offshore Books - Our friends in faraway places

Off the Board - A game bettors cannot wager on.

Opening Line – Where the oddsmakers make the original lines before the public money moves it.

Over - The combined score of two teams is more than what the sportsbook set.

Parlay - A bet that combines multiple games for a higher payout. The more games, the higher the risk but the greater the payout. In order for the parlay to win, each game must win or push (tie). If any of the games lose, the entire wager loses. Spoiler Alert: we recommend NEVER to play them.

Pick'em - A game with no favorite or underdog.

Point spread - Margin of victory set by oddsmakers to attract bets action on both the favorite and the underdog. A favorite must win by a number higher than the point spread to cover the spread. An underdog can cover by losing by a number less than the spread or by winning the game outright.

SIDE HUSTLE

Prop Bets (AKA Prop Culture) - A bet on anything that is not directly tied to the outcome of the game. For example, can Player A record more of less than X number of rushing yards in an NFL game.

Push - When neither team covers the spread (the actual margin of victory lands exactly on the spread), no one wins the bet and all wagers are refunded.

Runline - Baseball has a point spread of -1.5 for the favorite and +1.5 for the underdog.

Sharp AKA Wise Guy - A professional sports bettor.

Sports book – Where we make our bets in person (not via kiosk or app).

Steam - A quick change on a line due to heavy wagering.

Square AKA not so Wise Guy – An amateur sports bettor that doesn't profit long term.

Taking the points - Betting an underdog against the spread.

Teaser - Spreads are favored towards the bettor but has a lower payout.

Total bet AKA over/under - A bet on the combined number of points scored by both teams in a game, including overtime/extra innings.

SIDE HUSTLE

Under - The combined score of two teams is less than what the sportsbook set. Spoiler Alert: We love the unders.

Underdog AKA Dog - A team not favored to win a game. Spoiler Alert: We love the dogs!

Wager - A bet placed at a sportsbook.

www.ingramcontent.com/pod-product-compliance
Lightning Source LLC
LaVergne TN
LVHW061034070526
838201LV00073B/5033